Her Image of Salvation

Gender and the Biblical Tradition

Isis nursing Horus. From a terra-cotta figure, probably
Roman, ca. first or second century C.E.

Her Image of Salvation

Female Saviors and Formative Christianity

Gail Paterson Corrington

Westminster/John Knox Press
Louisville, Kentucky

Scripture quotations marked NRSV are from the New Revised Standard Version of the Bible, copyright © 1989 by the Division of Christian Education of the National Council of the Churches of Christ in the U.S.A., and are used by permission.

Scripture quotations marked NEB are taken from *The New English Bible,* © The Delegates of the Oxford University Press and The Syndics of the Cambridge University Press, 1961, 1970. Used by permission.

Frontispiece artwork is copyright © 1992 by Pem Pfisterer Clark and is used by permission.

Book design by Ken Taylor

First edition

Published by Westminster/John Knox Press
Louisville, Kentucky

This book is printed on acid-free paper that meets the American National Standards Institute Z39.48 standard. ∞

PRINTED IN THE UNITED STATES OF AMERICA
9 8 7 6 5 4 3 2 1

Library of Congress Cataloging-in-Publication Data

Corrington, Gail Paterson, 1949–
    Her image of salvation : female saviors and formative Christianity /
Gail Paterson Corrington. — 1st ed.
        p.   cm. — (Gender and the biblical tradition)
    Includes bibliographical references and index.
    ISBN 0-664-25389-X (pbk. : alk. paper)
    1. Salvation.   2. Femininity of God.   3. Sex—Religious aspects.
4. Jesus Christ—Person and offices.   5. Christianity—Origin.
I. Title.   II. Series.
BL476.C6 1992
234'.082—dc20   92-4360

To my mother,
Edith L. Paterson,
and in memory of my father,
Donald W. Paterson (1922–1983)

Contents

Preface

The gestation of this book has been a long one. Conceived during my graduate student days at Drew University in Madison, New Jersey, it remained an embryo until a number of midwives assisted its emergence. First and foremost, I would like to give heartfelt thanks to the Women's Program in Religion at Harvard Divinity School, for its funding of my research associateship in 1988–89, and to the program's director, Constance W. Buchanan. My students in the divinity school offered enthusiastic, challenging, and creative participation in my course, "The Female Redeemer," which I taught in the spring of 1989. They helped me to formulate and discuss many of the ideas contained in this book, and they deserve both credit and my thanks. I would also like to thank Carolyn DeSwarte Gifford, who was also a research associate at Harvard, for her comments, her conversation, and her company, not only on purely academic endeavors, but on forays into the North End of Boston and Kate's Mystery Bookstore in Cambridge, both of which provided welcome relief. The Department of New Testament at Harvard Divinity School; its students, especially Dan Schowalter, John Lanci, Georgia Frank, and Peggy Hutaff; and its faculty, especially Helmut Koester, Elisabeth Schüssler Fiorenza, Bernadette Brooten, Demetrius Trakatellis, and Laurence Wills, all assisted me in ways too numerous to mention. Margaret R. Miles, also of the divinity school faculty, deserves a special thanks for her sympathetic reading and insight-

9

ful comments on very early versions of this work. The Divinity School Library and its director, Charles Willard, also merit a special thanks and a remembrance of many hours I spent with the library's marvelous collections.

A second group of midwives at Rhodes College assisted the emergence of this creation, and to these I offer my thanks for their support, especially the Faculty Development Endowment Committee and the Dean of Academic Affairs, Harmon Dunathan, for the grant and other monetary support that funded the continued research and writing of this book. My wonderful colleagues at Rhodes also deserve more thanks than I have words to tell them, for many conversations on many levels, but primarily for being themselves. Special thanks, however, are due F. Michael McLain, Chairman of the Department of Religious Studies, and Valarie H. Ziegler, for their encouragement and for their friendship. Colleagues outside the department whose conversations and companionship have supported me throughout this research include Darlene Loprete, Michael Drompp, Charlotte McLain, Sandra McEntire, and the sisterhood of the Beatrice de Silva Society.

The members of the Ascetic Behavior in Greco-Roman Antiquity Group of the Society of Biblical Literature have remained my constant—though often geographically distant—colleagues, friends, and supporters. Those who make up this group, especially Vincent Wimbush (its director), Richard Valantasis, and Marilyn Nagy, have enriched, intrigued, entertained, and supported me for a number of years, and they have meant and still do mean a great deal to me, personally and professionally.

Last, but by no means least, I would like to thank my family, who, though absent, have been present with me in spirit and by the more mundane telephone; and my Siberian husky companion, Yukon Jack London II, for being his loyal, accepting, and warmly ubiquitous self.

Abbreviations

Periodicals, Series, and Collections

ANF   The Ante-Nicene Fathers

ATR   *Anglican Theological Review*

CBQ   *Catholic Biblical Quarterly*

EPRO   Études préliminaires aux religions orientales dans l'émpire romain

HR   *History of Religions*

HTR   *Harvard Theological Review*

IDB   *Interpreter's Dictionary of the Bible*

JNES   *Journal of Near Eastern Studies*

NTS   *New Testament Studies*

RevScRel   *Revue des sciences religieuses*

SBLDS   SBL Dissertation Series

SBLMS   SBL Monograph Series

SNTSMS   Society for New Testament Studies
                    Monograph Series

TDNT   *Theological Dictionary of the New
                    Testament*

Versions of the Bible

NEB   *The New English Bible*

NRSV   New Revised Standard Version

Her Image of Salvation

Introduction: Image Making and Image Taking

—What are we by nature?
—We are part of God's creation, made in the image of God.

—"Catechism," *The Book of Common Prayer* (1977)

Made in the Image?

Images and metaphors, as symbolic modes of discourse, help both to visualize and to interpret human experiences. Susanne K. Langer's work on symbolic forms, *Philosophy in a New Key* (1942), has emphasized the power of religious symbols to create images: They assist in the "envisagement of the essential pattern of human

15

life."[1] This pattern, expressed in language through metaphor and in art through visual image, gives shape and meaning—that is, embodiment—to human experiences. However, as Langer also has noted, although concepts are always thus metaphorically embodied, they may be so "rather too much."[2] The recent work of Sallie McFague on metaphor and theology has also stressed the hazards of the language of embodiment, observing that metaphors, when dominant or sustained, cease to function as acknowledged *symbolic* modes of expressing the reality in which they participate, and actually *shape* that reality, as models of what is assumed to be the "true" representation of "the way things are."[3] They become *models for,* rather than *models of,* human experience.[4] When models such as these have become further canonized (that is, embodied in the two formative bodies of canon in the West—the literature of the Greco-Roman world and the canon of biblical literature), they have not only presented certain received symbols, but they have assisted in formulating and continuing a tradition of "canonized conventions" that "evaluate *a priori* what we see."[5] Further, because "all historiography is a selective view of the past," images developed in the past will inevitably play a role in orienting the way persons "see" themselves and others in the present.[6]

In the symbolic language of religion particularly, the stakes are very high, for, as Margaret R. Miles has noted:

> The relative activity with which religious ideas and images are critically appropriated or the passivity with which they are intrajected seems to be crucial. . . . In using the religious ideas and images offered within their culture, women must choose carefully the religious symbols that effectively challenge and empower them rather than those that oppress and render them passive.[7]

It must be noted, however, that because of the link between power and representation, women traditionally have had little opportunity either for the development of images out of their own experiences or for choices among the images presented to them. Feminist critiques of literature and art therefore attempt "to expose that system of power that authorizes certain representations while blocking, prohibiting, or invalidating others."[8] These "others," while existing to be "recalled" from the repertoire of representation, are "forgotten" when chosen representations become dominant over time. Eventually, it becomes impossible even to visualize reality in terms of these forgotten images or metaphors, because the dominant representations themselves shape continued visualization. Hence, a dominant image, especially in religion, expresses the prevailing values of a society—or, to put it another way, the values of the dominant group in that society—when they are concretized in visual representations or embodied in texts. The problem of the selectivity of religious symbols and their relationships to dominance has been posed by Janet L. Nelson: "At a given moment, the religious tradition exists as a repertoire of symbols: why choose to employ some rather than others? And what determines the timing of the choice?"[9] Moreover, as Paul Minear has noted, images are not only the "possession of a community whose commerce over the centuries with the given reality has produced an extensive repertoire of effective images," but they also model an individual's "self-understanding" and "sense of direction."[10]

The religious traditions of Judaism and Christianity, by selecting certain images, particularly those for the deity, and by embodying them in their scriptures, have further sacralized and limited them, since each text is a "body" of images, images in a "body." Although the summary of the Law contained in the Ten Commandments expressly forbids, in the First Commandment, the making of images to represent the divine (Ex. 20:2), a prohibition continually reinforced by prophetic warnings, the deity is constantly embodied in images in the sacred text of the Tanak.[11] As Jacob Neusner has noted, "When portrayed as a personality, in any Judaism, God is represented in an incarnate way," which includes "allusions to God's corporeal form" and corporeal action.[12] The impossibility of visualizing the deity apart from metaphors drawn from human life is concretized in the first creation narrative in Genesis:

> And God (*Elohim*) created the human ('*adam*) in his
>   image (*tselem*);
> in the image of God created he him;
> male and female (*zakar v neqebah*) created he them.
>   (Gen. 1:27)[13]

As Paul Diel has expressed it, "Man created his idealized image, called 'God,' and the myth will say that man was created in the image of God."[14] "Woman" as the image of God, however, drops out of the repertoire of representations very quickly.

In the New Testament canon, the image of the deity has become twice embodied: in the person of Jesus of Nazareth and in the text that conveys certain images of this "image" of the divine. The word of God is made flesh in a particular way—in Jesus, who is also the "flesh" of the word (*kerygma*) that witnesses to him. The author of the epistle to the Hebrews puts this difference most succinctly:

> God, having spoken in the past in many fragmented
> and various ways to our ancestors in the prophets, to-
> wards the end of these days has spoken to us in a
> son, . . . the reflection (*apaugasma*) of his glory, the very
> stamp of his reality (*charackter tes hypostaseos*), sustaining
> all things by the word of his power. (Heb. 1:1–3)

The divine image, represented in two modes in Genesis 1:27, male and female, is here particularized in only one:

embodied in a person, the person of Jesus of Nazareth, and thus "localized" in this manifestation in a particular person, gender, place, and time. The universal has become particularized: *This* representation is seen as *the exact* and hence the *only* representation of the divine reality.

Such a particularizing of universals is a persistent tendency within the language of Western monotheism, which tends to limit representations of the deity while at the same time allowing for the deity's metaphorical personification. Paul Diel, writing from the perspective of anthropological Freudianism, sees personification as inevitable in the development of religious thinking, as in religious discourse: "Personification remains, even in the most evolved cultures, the root of all metaphorical truth, of all poetry."[15] The "danger" inherent in such symbolism, for Diel as for McFague, is in mistaking the "symbolic" personification of the subject for its "reality," or for "the lawful formation of the subject."[16]

The persistence and prevalence of a certain symbolic personification lead to an inability to perceive any other, equally symbolic, personifications as descriptive of reality. Once again, this inability or unavailability of choice is particularly noticeable in the Jewish and Christian stream of influence upon both verbal and visual imaging of deity in the West. This is the problem Rita M. Gross emphasizes in her treatment of feminine imagery for the deity in Jewish theology: When personal metaphors are used for a transcendent deity, they inevitably become gendered.[17] The problem becomes the more acute when the deity is seen, not merely as *personal*, but as a *person*. Because descriptive language is culturally conditioned, the attributes of such a person include those of gender. Therefore, as Judith Ochshorn has noted, the monotheism of Judaism and Christianity, by limiting the concept of the deity over time to a single, all-powerful personality, entails the assignment of one gender to that personality: historically, the gender that was perceived by the image makers as

the "less limited" and hence more "powerful" in its sociobiological roles.[18] The resultant gendered images seem
to their makers to be natural, inevitable, and representative of the "true"—that is, they are incapable of being
otherwise. In this way, as Diel observes, when the institutions governing the "inner life" of religion are no longer
the creatures of the "metaphysical vision" that created
them, but seize power themselves, they "stifle the emo-
tivity and motivation that gave birth to them."[19] Further,
as McFague notes, "The human images that are chosen
as metaphors for God gain in stature and take on divine
qualities by being placed in an interactive relationship
with the divine."[20]

In the Image of the Male: Jesus as Model of Savior and Saved

The present study, having developed out of issues like those delineated above, is therefore concerned
with two things: an image and an experience. The image
is that of the savior; the experience is that of salvation.
And because an image is formulated from and makes
reference to experience, the two are inextricably en-
twined. The present discussion is further concerned with
the dynamics of salvation in one particular religion of
salvation—Christianity—and with the way its particular
savior is imaged and envisioned. For Christianity, Jesus of
Nazareth is located in history as the one who announced
and put into practice the coming radical transformation of the world into the realm of justice willed by
God. But, as Rudolph Bultmann long ago noted, the
"proclaimer became the proclaimed,"[21] not only as the
symbolic embodiment of divine power, but even as the lit-

eral embodiment of that power through his conquest of death. Any investigation of Jesus as the savior must also therefore be concerned with the related concepts of salvation and redemption: how one is saved, and from what one is saved. Many other studies have dealt with the problem of having a single, personal, and therefore gendered deity; however, the tension between the universal (savior) and the particular (one savior: that is, Jesus) was not retained in Christianity, but was collapsed and forgotten. Language like that of the epistle to the Colossians links the language of salvation succinctly to the description of Christ as the "image" of God: Christ is he "in whom we have redemption, the remission of our sins: he is the image of the unseen God, the first born of the entire creation" (Col. 1:14–15). Because Christianity, like many of the religions of the Greco-Roman world in which it arose, developed primarily as a religion of salvation, the personality of the savior is extremely important. The image of the savior is the image of the saved, insofar as the agent of salvation models self-perception, self-orientation, and self-empowerment.

In this context, the question of gender, like all other questions of particularity, becomes important. As Mary Daly expressed it in *Beyond God the Father*: "The problem is not that the Jesus of the Gospels was male, young, and a Semite. Rather, the problem lies in the exclusive identification of this person with God, in such a manner that Christian conceptions of divinity and of the 'image' of God are all objectified in Jesus."[22] Because Jesus, a particular male, has been for Christianity not only the sole embodiment of the deity but also the sole redeemer and savior of flawed human existence, the relationship of women to Jesus, as the model of both the savior and saved existence, is problematic. As Rosemary R. Ruether posed the question, "Can a male savior save women?"[23] Daly also has expressed this idea in her "Feminist Post-Christian Introduction" to *The Church and the Second Sex* (1985), noting that she herself had originally "missed the point about the Christ symbol"; Daly says that when she criticized Roman Catholic theologians who insisted the priest must be male and who gave "prior importance to [Christ's] maleness rather than his humanity," she forgot that Christ's maleness *was* the point.[24] Ruether, in *Women-Church*, did not miss the connection between the maleness of Jesus and his adoption as a savior figure by the church hierarchy:

> Who is this savior, and from what does he save us? This savior of men comes to free men from birth, from women, from earth, and from limits. This savior can only come in the image of the male. As God can only be imaged as male, as the male is the proper image of God, so the savior too must be male. . . . Only the male represents perfect humanity. In turn, only the male can represent Christ.[25]

Ruether critiques what she considers the misappropriation of the "symbol of Christian theology that should manifest the face of God/ess as liberator, . . . disclosing, at one and the same time, the gracious, redeeming face of God/ess and our authentic potential."[26] This critique reflects the process of development whereby Christian persons "image" themselves in some sense as Christ, since they participate in his humanity as he participates in theirs. Paul had already expressed this sense of participation in his discussion of the "first" and "last" Adam in 1 Corinthians 15:49: "And just as we have borne the image of the man of earth, we shall also bear the image of the man of heaven." Then how would or did Christian women see themselves as Christ, or Christ as themselves? Bernadette Brooten has phrased the question in this way: "Are New Testament concepts of God, redeemer, salvation, ethics, etc. adequate to an understanding of humanity which emphasizes the equal dignity and equal rights of men and women?"[27] As Brooten has noted, answering this question is especially difficult because there is nothing from the New Testament itself that recounts "women's theological and ethical reflections and their own account of their experiences."[28]

Because of this paucity of canonical evidence, it may be fruitful to turn to a noncanonical source—the apocryphal Acts—to find some indication of how Christian women were seen as following the model of Jesus in early Christianity. As an example, let us examine a particular image of Jesus that appears in the New Testament and early Christianity: that of the divine man (*theios aner*). While all of the canonical New Testament writers treat Jesus as a model for the Christian (although each does it from a different perspective), the model of the miracle-working charismatic seems to be that which most thoroughly grasped the popular imagination.[29] This is the model for discipleship adopted in the canonical book of Acts, but it also appears in virtually the same pattern in the noncanonical books of Acts, in which miracle working has been combined with ascetic practice. One of the more fascinating aspects of the apocryphal Acts is the number of miracle-working ascetic women who appear as heroines and models for the behavior of female Christians.[30]

In reading these stories, it is easy to be distracted by the portrayal of these women as powerful and apparently autonomous and to overlook the model that they are following. By rejecting the socially mandated roles of wifehood and motherhood, these women are patterning themselves after models of power and autonomy available in their world and in its literature: the male apostles, who in turn are patterned on the model of Christ. Of the three possible avenues of women's spiritual empowerment within the early Christian world—enthusiasm (female prophecy), asceticism, and martyrdom—the latter two involve "becoming male," achieving a spiritual manliness through the denial of female embodiment.[31] The first route—enthusiasm, "being filled with the divine," of which the prophetesses of Apollo and the maenads of Dionysus are both models—appears to have been rejected early on in Christianity because of its problematic relationship to a female sexuality perceived as "uncontrolled."

In the other two dominant expressions of women's spiritual empowerment, martyrdom and asceticism, female sexuality and the socially determined image of the female body are not merely denied but "overcome." These are examples of "making oneself male." In one of the most important first-person narratives of martyrdom, and the only one by a woman, the third-century *Martyrdom of Saints Perpetua and Felicitas,* for example, the narrator, Vibia Perpetua, has terminated all of her social roles as daughter, sister, wife, and mother. Her choosing Christianity has made her sever her ties with her father; her brother (whom she saves in a dream) is dead; her husband does not appear in the picture; and early in her imprisonment she has sent away her nursing son, so that her breast-milk dries up. While imprisoned, Perpetua dreams that she is being prepared for an athletic contest against an "Egyptian," a metaphor for the devil. To prepare for the contest, she becomes a man, and only as a male athlete is she victorious. She sees herself in conquest as a man. Thus, both in Perpetua's earthly and in her heavenly life, her models of authority and power are not female, but all male.

The model for the ascetic woman was also a male model. In all of the stories of women in the apocryphal Acts, for example, women reject all social roles that identify and limit them as women, especially the role of wife. The heroine of the popular second-century apocryphal *Acts of Paul and Thecla,* converted by the apostle Paul's "word of the chaste life," refuses her fiancé, is condemned to burning as an "unbride" at the instigation of her mother, but miraculously escapes this and other trials, usually taking the form of threats to her virginity. She finally cuts her hair and dons male clothing, conforming to her model, the apostle Paul, who confirms her apostolic "freedom." One of the so-called harlot saints, Pelagia, marked her conversion to Christianity by dressing as a man and passing as a male monk until her death. Amma Sarah, one of the desert mothers, was herself a model for male monks, but claimed that while her sex was that of a woman, her spirit was male.[32] Even Gnostic Christians, regarded as heretics by those orthodox Christians who also valued celibacy, spoke of females "making themselves male" in order to enter the kingdom of heaven.[33] For Paul, all Christians had "put on" Christ in baptism (Gal. 3:27–28), and Christians, male and female, wore the "image" of Christ, the second Adam (1 Cor. 15:50); in contrast, by the time of Methodius in the third century, baptism had become a "virgin birth" in which the believers became, like Christ, specifically male: "The enlightened receive the features and the image and the manliness of Christ" (*Symposium* 8.7).

Is this clear valuation of the male over the female in formative Christianity the result of envisioning the Christian savior as male, or is it a mere historical accident that Jesus the messiah was male? It has been argued that the perceived revelation of deity in the particular person of Jesus of Nazareth might yet be maintained as a "metaphor," while the understanding of that "person" of the deity be expanded or redefined so that this person could be seen as a "feminist" in action, as "androgynous" in nature, as a means by which male and female are united in the "body of Christ," or as a person who transcends personality and thus is the "alternate male/female."[34] All of these strategies of seeing and therefore saving Jesus as the savior have been proposed, but that there are difficulties in each strategy is undeniable. A critique of the first position, which she herself once held, is offered by Daly: "What sense does it make to assert that *in Christ* 'there is neither male nor female'? Wasn't 'Christ' an exclusively male symbol, even though somewhat 'feminized'?"[35] Of Jesus as the "image of the androgyne," Naomi Goldenberg points out that such a symbol, both for the deity and for humanity, has proven historically "unworkable," and is fundamentally unsatisfactory in that it has failed to take account of the full reality of the female component of the androgyne, which is submerged *in* the male, not merged *with* it.[36] The failure of the personal God to transcend the duality male/female has been noted already, while a Christ figure who "transcends" such duality, as Paul Tillich envisioned the concept, does not simply incorporate "the female element," which has been particularly slighted by Protestant Christianity, lest it, in Tillich's view, render the Christ figure "effeminate."[37] Thus the female is rigidly excluded from the personae of the deity, and at the same time femaleness is devalued as an appropriate personal attribute of the deity. The alternate to a male persona is an asexual rather than a bisexual or androgynous being, which results from the rejection of the female gender and female sexuality, in preference for the male. Once again, because of a particular historical situation, other possible metaphorical truths cannot be seen.

Because there is a sense of inevitability about the gender of the savior, as traditionally perceived by Christianity, a statement is thus also made regarding the incarnational or bodily aspect of the savior, the bodies of the saved and their respective sexes, and the role gender plays in the responsibility for the "flaw" that made salvation necessary. During the formative centuries of Christianity, the second to the fourth, the great debates concerning the extent of the humanity (embodiment) of Jesus tended also to involve the human being from whom he was perceived as having derived his humanity, his mother Mary. Although such controversies may be seen as debates over Jesus Christ as part of the godhead, with Mary as a secondary consideration, they nevertheless reveal important attitudes about incarnation and the almost universal identification of the female with flesh, flesh with birth, birth with death, and, therefore, in the Christian economy of salvation, with sin, of which death is the consequence (Rom. 6:23). The shrill insistence of many of the church fathers on the issue of Mary's virginity before, during, and after the birth of Jesus may be regarded as attempts to rescue the male savior from the taint of fallen flesh, which was increasingly perceived by early Christian writers as being linked to the female. Irenaeus of Lyons linked Mary to Eve as Paul had earlier linked Christ to Adam. In an exegesis of the first chapter of Luke, Irenaeus defends both Jesus' virgin birth and the untainted flesh that he took from Mary:

> [Eve], having become disobedient, was made the cause of death, both to herself and to the entire human race; so also did Mary, having a man betrothed [to her] and being nevertheless a virgin, by yielding obedience, become the cause of salvation, both to herself and the whole human race. . . . And thus also it was that the knot of Eve's disobedience was loosed by the obedience of Mary. For what the virgin Eve had bound fast through unbelief, this did the virgin Mary set free through faith. (*Against Heresies* 22.3–4)[38]

The startling implication of this passage, that Mary has redeemed not only herself but the whole of humanity, must be set aside for the moment to consider the role being female plays in the rhetoric of salvation. There appears in the patristic tradition the concept of a fundamental flaw in the female nature and in female physicality and sexuality that predisposes women particularly to limitation, imperfection, and disobedience. Because these characteristics seemed to be located within the female body, it was impossible within the early Christian tradition to visualize particular female persons as the embodiment of the divine. While women could certainly be seen as the appropriate object (*focus*) of redemption and salvation, a woman or women could not be seen as the primary or appropriate source (*locus*) of redeeming and saving power. As Peter Brown has so cogently demonstrated in his study of the problematic of sexuality in early

Christianity, the great emphasis on control of the body, derived in large part from the tradition of Greco-Roman male thought, was the result of an equally great anxiety about the limitations of the body, and women's bodies in particular appeared to be "limited" by the "manifest discontinuities" of menstruation and childbirth.[39] Moreover, the manifest "bodiliness" of women enabled men to view women as *the* body, an unruly "other" whose tendency toward being "out of control" was a persistent source of anxiety.

Perhaps for this reason, the Genesis creation story continued to fascinate early Christian theologians who sought a solution to the problem of embodied existence: its limitation and especially its limitation by death. The hellenized Jewish exegete Philo allegorized the two creation stories as indicative of two natures of humanity: The first nature was spiritual, and the spirit was the "image" of the deity; the second was physical, "of the earth," and therefore subject to imperfection and decay.[40] The hellenized Jewish exegete Paul likewise employed the two creations in his Adam/Christ typology of 1 Corinthians 15:21–22 and Romans 5:12–19. In both passages, and particularly in the latter, the persons of Adam and Christ are metaphors for the persons of the saved:

> Therefore, then, just as through one offense there is judgment against all persons, so also through one righteous act there is the acquittal of life for all persons. For just as through the disobedience of one person the many have become sinners, so also through the obedience of one person the many shall become just. (Rom. 5:18–19)

The language of this passage is echoed by Irenaeus in the above-mentioned passage on the Eve/Mary typology.

As a female symbol, Eve plays a major part in the early Christian economy of salvation, a part that virtually creates the necessity for Mary's role, as Adam's did for Christ's. In the Hebrew scriptures, the figure of Eve virtually disappears after the third chapter of Genesis, and she equally plays very little role in the Jewish literature of the second century B.C.E. and later, except for some of the pseudepigraphical works, like the *Apocalypse of Moses* and the *Book of the Secrets of Enoch* (*2 Enoch*), books that appear to have exercised quite an influence upon the Christian patriarchs.[41] But as Cynthia Ozick has observed, Eve became essential to Christianity:

> Eve's "sin" leads to Adam's "fall." The Fall of Man is not a Jewish notion; it is purely Christian. And without the Fall, there would be no need for Redemption; and without a need for Redemption, there would be no Crucified Christ and no Vicarious Atonement. In short, for Christianity, if you take Eve out of Scripture, Christianity itself vanishes.[42]

Although her point is stated perhaps too emphatically (after all, the Rabbis developed Adam's mythic first wife, Lilith, to explain demonic female corruption; and the need for redemption is not an unknown in Judaism), Ozick does not exaggerate the importance of Eve for early Christian theologies of redemption.

To explain this importance and its role in Christian soteriology, we must return to the idea of the dual creation of humanity. While Paul employed the dual creation as a metaphorical description of the two "natures" of humanity, he also could use it to justify the control of one gender by the other, symbolized by the veiling of married women prophets in the worship services at Corinth: "A man therefore, does not have to cover his head, being the image and glory of God. A woman, however, is the glory of man. Man was not made from woman, but woman from man" (1 Cor. 11:7–8). In this passage, to be woman is to be the second-created human being, symbolizing the lower order of creation, further from the image of God. Paul, then, shared the predisposition of his

Gentile, male contemporaries, who regarded the female
as the symbol of imperfection, and he held the viewpoint they shared with his Jewish contemporaries, who
tended to see the female as the symbol of unruly sexuality that needed careful control. He did not, however,
make extensive use either of Eve as the corporate symbol of female humanity or of the narrative of the Fall in
Genesis 3 as justifying the need for continued control of
unruly womankind.

Paul's disciples developed the idea of a hierarchy of creation and turned it into a virtual hierarchy of salvation.
For Paul, the act of salvation took place in the "putting
on" of Christ and thus of the person of Christ as the victor
over both sin and death (Gal. 3:26–28). This corporate
and incorporated "person," with many members, had no
differentiation into genders or social statuses. But even
Paul could not preserve this attitude in all situations, especially those in which the activities of Christians might
bring them into conflict with those who held authority
in the "world," as the passage from 1 Corinthians 11:2–
16, noted above, demonstrates. Further, in the face of
constant pressure to accommodate existing social norms,
Paul's followers were even less able to preserve the apocalyptic and sectarian stance of communities who often saw
themselves as living now "the life to come."[43] Thus, in
1 Timothy 2:11–15, written in the early second century,
we find—in connection with advice on the necessity for
women to remain "modestly" attired and with a call for
silence and submissiveness—a reiteration of Paul's reference to the "order" of creation, but now further justified
by the responsibility of Eve, "the woman," for the Fall:

> Let woman remain in silence in every form of submis-
> sion. I do not permit a woman to teach, nor to hold
> authority over a man, but to be quiet. For Adam was
> created first, then Eve. And Adam was not deceived,
> but the woman, having been deceived, fell into sin.
> (1 Tim. 2:11–14)

This hierarchy of creation now entails a hierarchy of salvation: The "woman," who now bears chief responsibility for the Fall, "will be saved through childbearing [or, the childbearing], if she remains in faith and love and holiness with self-control [or chastity]" (1 Tim. 2:15). Thus, the price women must pay for Eve's sin is heavy. No longer is Adam (representing corporate humanity) responsible for the Fall; it is Eve (corporate womankind) who is responsible. Even the "vicarious atonement" of Christ is not enough to redeem women: Their salvation needs further work.

We return, then, to the question with which we began this section: Can a male savior save women? A related question that might be asked is: Why must the savior be male? In Christian terms, this question must necessarily involve how the figure of Jesus as savior is portrayed. Paula Fredriksen has noted that the texts of the New Testament "are concerned to portray, and to communicate the unique significance of the figure of Jesus." The images that are chosen for this purpose reflect not only the Hellenistic world, pagan and Jewish, but also the specific language of "Jewish restoration theology," which envisions the restoration of Israel along with the redemption of the world by the establishment of God's (YHWH's) reign.[44] These canonical images were often forged in competition with each other and certainly in competition with understandings of personal and corporate transformation—salvation—in the surrounding world.[45] What was unique about Jesus as savior was necessarily spoken of in the language of images from that surrounding world, to make an appeal to its various constituencies.

The path to salvation, presented by the traditions embedded in the Gospels, was manifold. However, the dialogue between Jesus and the rich man, told in its simplest form in Mark 10:17–30, with parallels in Matthew 19:16–29 and Luke 19:18–30, revolves around the question of the means by which eternal life, or life in the age of restoration to come, may be attained. The man asks the popular preacher a question that preoccupied Jewish piety of the first century,[46] "What must I do to obtain a share in eternal life?" (Mark 10:17). In keeping with the developing rabbinic tradition, Jesus' reply first stresses the importance of observing the Commandments. But he goes on to urge a further step that is in keeping with his own radical vision of eschatological renewal: The man is to divest himself of the property that ties him to the world, just as any disciple must give up social and familial ties (see Mark 10:29–30). Jesus invites the man, "Come and follow me" (Mark 10:21). Quite apart from the question of renunciation, one that was to have a continuing and almost obsessive importance for ascetic Christian movements of the second to fourth centuries, the emphasis in this passage is upon discipleship or "following." One "follows" the model of Jesus himself in order to attain a share in eternal life.

Certainly none of the acrimonious arguments over whether women can be admitted to the clergy, continuing from the second century (or possibly earlier) until the present, would have taken place had it been clear that gender, among other social constructs like the family, was eschatologically unimportant, or if the life of Jesus had been understood purely as a metaphor for the life of the disciple. In the latter case particularly, the gender of Jesus would not have been an important part of the model to be followed. But the gender of Jesus *has* historically been quite an important aspect of his person, precisely *as* savior and redeemer and as the model for those who wished to be saved. Even though women were included in the group of persons originally associated with Jesus' renewal movement and were urged to give up their socially constructed roles for the sake of the kingdom of God, as were all disciples,[47] one of the very passages that has frequently been used to illustrate this radical eschatological inclusiveness, that of Mary and Martha in Luke 10:38–41, contains some disturbing implications of the way in which women are seen as disciples. In this story,

Martha is the model of the disciple who is too preoccupied with fulfilling her social function of "service" to choose "the good part." Mary, in contrast, as the model of the ideal disciple, sits at the feet of the famous teacher. While many interpretations of this story are possible, I wish to focus on the aspect of gender as illustrated by Mary as the model disciple. I believe that this story is far from indicating the equality of men and women as disciples in the kingdom of God. Although the confinement of women to service roles does appear to be rejected in the case of Martha, Mary's actions are not illustrative of inclusiveness of women in the community that celebrates the inauguration of the kingdom of God, but of a woman taking on a male role: the male student "sitting at the feet" of the male rabbi. As in the case of asceticism and martyrdom, women must become men in order to be saved.[48] A male savior can save women only if they become men: that is, if they pattern their behavior after a dominant male model that does not partake of their own experience. Mary's choice of "the good part," therefore, means not seeing herself as a female. The *Gospel of Thomas* (second century), although coming from Gnostic Christianity, contains a passage that well illustrates this ironic "choice." That passage is Jesus' famous reply to Peter's objection to the discipleship of Mary Magdalene and to Peter's comment on the unworthiness of women for "the life." Jesus states: "See, I am going to attract her to make her male so that she too might become a living spirit that resembles you males. For every female (element) that makes itself male will enter the kingdom of heavens" (*Gospel of Thomas* 114).[49]

Having indicated the importance of Jesus' gender in his role as savior, let us offer some possible ways in which that role can be envisioned. First, according to Paul, by following the model of Jesus and by participating in Jesus as Christ, one can attain eternal life: that is, "be saved." Hence, one image of Jesus Christ is as the universal savior, participation in whom guarantees eternal life. That model comes largely from the Greco-Roman world. Second, Jesus can be seen as a teacher who both imparts and embodies divine Wisdom as a part of God. Thus a second image of Jesus Christ is that of Wisdom (Sophia or Logos), the mediating figure between the divine and human realms.

Finally, both images are aspects of a third concept: the incarnation or embodiment of the divine in a human person. Jesus Christ is thus the image not only of the redeemer, but of redeemed humanity. It is my contention that none of these images necessarily requires a male savior, but that such a soteriology was developed and embedded in Christianity in such a way that neither the savior nor the saved could be seen as female. In order to prove this contention, these three "images"—universal savior who overcomes death, embodied Wisdom who mediates between the divine and the human realms, and deity incarnate—will be explored with reference to female saving personae in comparison with Jesus. The universal savior will be represented by the Hellenistic goddess Isis, who saves both men and women precisely because she is female: the creator, redeemer, and sustainer of human life. The comparison between Jesus and Isis will center upon their different modes of saving. Many of Isis's attributes are ascribed to the second female persona, Wisdom (Hokhmah/Sophia), who is the mediator between the divine and human realms, as traditionally seen in Jewish canonical and extracanonical wisdom literature. In Gnostic Christian scriptures, moreover, the figure of Sophia is the model both of the fallen and redeemed soul and of the redeemer. For orthodox Christianity, and in the New Testament, particularly the Gospel of John, the female, divine hypostasis—that is, Wisdom—becomes "realized" in the male Jesus as the Logos. Finally, a third alternative will be presented: If the "image of God" is created in two genders—male and female—then God can be seen as incarnate in a female person. In this context, Mary of Nazareth will be contrasted to Jesus, not merely as the "vehicle of salvation," but as herself a possible savior.

Context and Method

In terms of historical context, this study must necessarily begin with the historical period of formative Christianity, which both coalesces in and develops out of the canon of the New Testament and which ranges from the Hellenistic period (fourth century B.C.E.) to the time at which Christianity began to dominate the religious life of the Roman Empire (fourth century C.E.). The reason for choosing this particular time period is that, in Christianity, the two broad streams of Judaism and Greco-Roman religiosity come together, and, when merged with the political and social systems of power in the Roman Empire, this particular synthesis, with its accompanying images, has had a dominant role in Western cultural history, for good or ill. Many feminists in the West have rejected not only Judaism and Christianity, but also their symbol-structures, as embodied in the texts of the Hebrew scriptures and the New Testament, because they give privilege to and validate a patriarchal structure and an androcentric perspective that must be eliminated in order to see things anew. While not disagreeing with the view that a great many oppressive systems of power (not only in terms of gender, ethnic, and racial ideologies) are privileged by this particular canon, I agree with Elisabeth Schüssler Fiorenza's statement that feminists ignore the symbolic universe embedded in these texts at their peril, even when they wish to construct an alternative: "Feminists cannot afford such an ahistorical or antihistorical stance because it is precisely the power of oppression that deprives people of their history."[50] Discovering their heritage is one of the ways for those who have been traditionally oppressed and excluded to see strategies both of empowerment and disempowerment within their own cultural, religious, and social histories. I also agree with Phyllis Trible to the extent that she would not have feminist biblical scholars emphasizing models of women's empowerment only, at the expense of not seeing and therefore not remembering as part of their heritage the disempowered, who are thereby robbed both of voice and of history.[51] The method this study will follow, therefore, needs to take into account, as far as possible, the origination, development, and transformation—even the tyranny—of the metaphorical language of salvation and possible images of the savior within formative Christianity. Although this perspective has to do mainly with the language of image, metaphor, and model, it must necessarily operate also within the larger paradigm of history, of which religion forms an obvious and often controlling part. This study will also be concerned with the role of gender in the language and symbolic personifications of salvation, especially as conveyed in the biblical texts and those closely related to them.

The method of this study owes much to the work of Sallie McFague on the use of metaphor and model in religious language, particularly her *Metaphorical Theology*. Within my discussion, the term *image* is used to refer to a metaphor, verbal or visual, which, although idealizing a particular reality or experience, participates in it. Following McFague, I also understand the term *model* to denote a metaphor or image that has become dominant over time and thus not only assists in the explanation and description of reality, but also shapes the perception of that reality and behavior within it. I will use the term *paradigm* to denote a framework of a traditional "way of seeing" within which models and metaphors operate as symbolic modes of description. In the present study, there are two major and related frameworks or paradigms in which models of the savior and of the saved operate: the paradigms of salvation and of redemption. Let us now turn to these paradigms and their development within the varied contexts of biblical Judaism and New Testament Christianity.

Notes

1. Susanne K. Langer, *Philosophy in a New Key: A Study in the Symbolism of Reason, Rite, and Art* (Cambridge, Mass.: Harvard University Press, 1942), 155.

2. Ibid., 61 n. 6.

3. Sallie McFague, *Metaphorical Theology: Models of God in Religious Language* (Philadelphia: Fortress Press, 1981), 74.

4. Clifford Geertz, "Religion as a Cultural System," in *Anthropological Approaches to the Study of Religion*, ed. Michael Banton (London and New York: Tavistock Publications, 1966), 1–46.

5. Martha L. Banta, *Imaging American Women: Idea and Ideals in Cultural History* (New York: Columbia University Press, 1987), xxx.

6. Elisabeth Schüssler Fiorenza, *In Memory of Her: A Feminist Theological Reconstruction of Christian Origins* (New York: Crossroad, 1983), xviii.

7. Margaret R. Miles, "Introduction," in *Immaculate and Powerful: The Female in Sacred Image and Social Reality*, ed. Clarissa W. Atkinson, Constance W. Buchanan, and Margaret R. Miles (Boston: Beacon Press, 1985), 2. Miles has indicated to me that, because of the connection between selectivity of images and power, she no longer believes this choice is possible.

8. Craig R. Owens, "The Discourse of Others: Feminists and Post-modernism," in *The Anti-aesthetic: Essays in Post-modern Culture*, ed. Hal Foster (Port Townsend, Wash.: Bag Press, 1983), 57–77.

9. Janet L. Nelson, "Society, Theodicy, and the Origins of Medieval Heresy," in *Schism, Heresy, and Religious Protest*, ed. D. Baker (Cambridge: Cambridge University Press, 1972), 68.

10. Paul Minear, *Images of the Church in the New Testament* (Philadelphia: Westminster Press, 1966), 23–24.

11. An acronym for the Hebrew scriptures: Torah, Nevi'im, and Ketubim, used in preference to the Christian term, Old Testament.

12. Jacob Neusner, *The Incarnation of God: The Character of Divinity in Formative Judaism* (Philadelphia: Fortress Press, 1988), 1.

13. Where a specific translation is not indicated, the translation is my own.

14. Paul Diel, *The God-Symbol: Its History and Its Significance*, trans. Nelly Marans (San Francisco: Harper & Row, 1986), 83.

15. Ibid., 61.

16. Ibid., 59–61; McFague, *Metaphorical Theology,* 74.

17. Rita M. Gross, "Steps Toward Feminine Imagery of Deity in Jewish Theology," in *On Being a Jewish Feminist,* ed. Susannah Heschel (New York: Schocken Books, 1983), 236.

18. Judith Ochshorn, *The Female Experience and the Nature of the Divine* (Bloomington, Ind.: Indiana University Press, 1981), 136–40.

19. Diel, *God-Symbol,* 59.

20. McFague, *Metaphorical Theology,* 38.

21. Rudolf Bultmann, *Jesus Christ and Mythology* (London: SCM Press, 1961).

22. Mary Daly, *Beyond God the Father: Toward a Philosophy of Women's Liberation* (Boston: Beacon Press, 1973), 78–79.

23. Rosemary R. Ruether, "Can a Male Savior Save Women?" in *Sexism and God-Talk: Toward a Feminist Theology* (Boston: Beacon Press, 1983), 116–34.

24. Mary Daly, "Feminist Post-Christian Introduction," in *The Church and the Second Sex* (Boston: Beacon Press, 1985), 120.

25. Rosemary R. Ruether, *Women-Church: Theology and Practice of Feminist Liberation Communities* (San Francisco: Harper & Row, 1985), 70.

26. Ibid., 70; see also Ruether, *Womanguides: Readings Toward a Feminist Theology* (Boston: Beacon Press, 1985), x.

27. Bernadette Brooten, "Feminist Perspectives on New Testament Exegesis," *Concilium* 138 (1980): 55.

28. Ibid., 56.

29. A fuller exploration of this model and its popularity will be found in capsule form in my article "Power and the Man of

Power in Hellenistic Popular Belief," *Helios*, n.s., 13/1 (1986): 75–86, and in my *The "Divine Man": His Origin and Function in Hellenistic Popular Religion*, American University Studies, 8:17 (Bern and New York: Peter Lang, 1986).

30. There are a growing number of studies of the roles of women in the apocryphal Acts as models of and for women's behavior. See, for example, Virginia Burrus, "Chastity as Autonomy: Women in the Stories of the Apocryphal Acts," in *The Apocryphal Acts of the Apostles*, ed. Dennis R. MacDonald, Semeia, 38 (Decatur, Ga.: Scholars Press, 1986), 105–118; and my "The Divine Woman: A Reconsideration," *ATR* 70/3 (July 1988): 207–20.

31. See, for example, Margaret R. Miles, "Becoming Male," in *Carnal Knowing* (Boston: Beacon Press, 1989), 53–77.

32. See my "Divine Woman: A Reconsideration" and "The Milk of Salvation: Redemption by the Mother in Late Antiquity and Early Christianity," *HTR* 82/4 (July 1989): 393–420; and Miles, "Becoming Male," 53–77. Although both my articles and the chapter by Miles use the same or similar examples, they were written entirely independently.

33. See *The Gospel of Mary*, in *The Nag Hammadi Library in English*, ed. James M. Robinson (San Francisco: Harper & Row, 1977), 472; *The Gospel of Thomas*, logion 114, in *The Gnostic Scriptures*, trans. Bentley Layton (Garden City, N.Y.: Doubleday, 1987), 399.

34. For these positions, in their respective order of citation, see McFague, *Metaphorical Theology;* Leonard Swidler, "Jesus Was a Feminist," *Catholic World* 214 (1971): 177–83; Wayne Meeks, "The Image of the Androgyne," *HR* 13 (1974): 165–208; and Paul Tillich, *Systematic Theology* (Chicago: University of Chicago Press, 1963), 3:294.

35. Daly, *Beyond God the Father,* 23.

36. Naomi Goldenberg, *The Changing of the Gods* (Boston: Beacon Press, 1979), 79.

37. Tillich, *Systematic Theology,* 3:294. Here Tillich, perhaps unwittingly, follows the above-mentioned "canonized conventions," formed by a long tradition of writers, pagan and Christian, who were always on guard lest the "female" element, symbolizing a lack of control, especially of the sexual variety, render the male element "effeminate" and hence "weak" (uncontrolled).

38. Translated in ANF, 1:454–55.
39. Peter Brown, *The Body and Society: Men, Women, and Sexual Renunciation in Early Christianity* (New York: Columbia University Press, 1988), 25–27.
40. See Philo, especially *On the Creation of the World* 136–72; *Questions on Genesis* 1.27.
41. See, for example, Bernard F. Prusak, "Woman: Seductive Siren and Source of Sin?" in *Religion and Sexism: Images of Women in the Jewish and Christian Traditions*, ed. Rosemary R. Ruether (New York: Simon & Schuster, 1974), 84–116, for a provocative discussion of the pseudepigraphical sources of the Fathers' obsession with Eve as a symbol.
42. Cynthia Ozick, "Notes Toward Finding the Right Question," in Heschel, ed., *On Being a Jewish Feminist*, 123.
43. For a persuasive and careful study of this development, see Schüssler Fiorenza, *In Memory of Her*, especially 205–41.
44. Paula Fredriksen, *From Jesus to Christ: The Origins of the New Testament Images of Jesus* (New Haven, Conn., and London: Yale University Press, 1988), 1‑8. "YHWH" represents the transliteration of the (unpronounceable) name of God in the Tanak; it is often spelled "Yahweh."
45. Ibid., 135.
46. Shaye Cohen, *From the Maccabees to the Mishnah*, Library of Early Christianity (Philadelphia: Westminster Press, 1987), 93–94.
47. See Schüssler Fiorenza, *In Memory of Her*, 145–51.
48. Some of this interpretation is based on the one offered by Elisabeth Schüssler Fiorenza, *Theological Criteria and Historical Reconstruction: Martha and Mary in Luke 10:38–42*, Center for Hermeneutical Studies, Protocol of the 53rd Colloquy, 10 April 1986 (Berkeley, Calif.: Graduate Theological Union and the University of California Press, 1987). However, while both interpretations emphasize the importance of gender in this passage, they interpret it in essentially different ways.
49. Layton, trans., *Gnostic Scriptures*, 399.
50. Schüssler Fiorenza, *In Memory of Her*, xix.
51. Phyllis Trible, *Texts of Terror* (Philadelphia: Fortress Press, 1985), 3.

1

What Must I Do
to Be Saved?
Receiving Salvation

> For us men and for our salvation,
> he came down from heaven,
> and was made man.
> —The Nicene Creed

The Discourse of Salvation

Christianity may be understood first as a Jewish sect with an apocalyptic perspective, looking toward
and prophetically enacting the radical transformation
of the world that would come about with the establishment of the reign of YHWH. Although this movement
was born in rural Palestinian Judaism, it increasingly

needed to deal with a world that was dominated by
the Greek language and cultural institutions and by
Roman political power. It was gradually transformed
into a "new" religion that took its place among other
religions of the Greco-Roman world. The symbolic universe of Christianity, therefore, includes and responds
to symbols operative within apocalyptic Judaism, hellenized Judaism, and Greco-Roman religiosity. Within
these systems of belief, two major paradigms emerge for
understanding human existence in the world. These are
the paradigms of salvation and its related but not always identical term, redemption. While it would not be
correct to limit the concept of salvation to Gentile religiosity and assign the concept of redemption solely to
Judaism, it is nevertheless the case that the idea of redemption did develop first in Judaism as a mode of
understanding salvation and was difficult to translate into
a Gentile, Hellenistic context. We can also assume that
the dominant expressions of these experiences will be
somewhat different for each religious tradition. Both salvation and redemption, however we may define them,
will necessarily involve the experience itself, including the perception of the situation *from* which one is
saved or redeemed, and, most importantly, *agency*, the
means through which redemption and salvation are effected. How does the *need* for redemption or salvation
arise? How is it perceived? From what or from whom
does one need to be saved, and how is one saved?
A concept of agency, moreover, must necessarily imply
receptivity: Who are those to be saved or redeemed?
Is salvation or redemption different for different persons? Therefore, within each paradigm we may expect
to find models of the redeemer/savior and of the re-
deemed/saved. This section of the discussion will focus
upon symbolic expressions of the experience of salvation and redemption in the religions of the Hellenistic
and early imperial periods (fourth century B.C.E. to second century C.E.), especially as they relate to the biblical

witness and particularly as they include questions of gender.

No matter how the historical and theological development and range of interpretations of the experience of salvation within the biblical world may be debated, the broadest understanding of the term *salvation* denotes an experience of the establishment (or reestablishment) of health, safety, or security that is accomplished *from the outside*, primarily in the face of threats from one or more hostile powers. A similar pattern obtains in expressions of the experience of *redemption*. The dominant model of redemption within Judaism, however nuanced and modified, has been that of the exodus from Egypt. This action is the foremost experience of divine deliverance from hostile powers and in fact provides the self-identification of Israel's God: "I am YHWH your God, who brought you out of the land of Egypt, to be your God: I am YHWH your God" (Num. 15:41, NRSV, modified). The importance of this action is such that it is held to be paradigmatic for the entire relationship of Israel to its deity, for individual Israelites as well as the nation itself: In effect, what is God for Israel is primarily defined in this action.[1] But this act of redemption, achieved by a powerful divine agent, entails an imperative. Amos expressed the prophetic understanding of the consequences of divine redemption for the people redeemed, an understanding that is dominant in the Hebrew scriptures (the Tanak):

> Hear this word that YHWH has spoken against you, O people of Israel, against the whole family that I brought up out of the land of Egypt:
> You only have I known
>   of all the families of the earth;
> therefore I will punish you
>   for all your iniquities.
>   (Amos 3:1–2, NRSV, modified)

In literary and scriptural expressions of salvation, the same pattern of rescue or deliverance from hostile powers by another power obtains. The ability to preserve corporate and individual life was so linked to an extra-mundane power, especially in the Greek and later the Roman mind, that it was associated with the divine. Only the divine, whether located in the heavens or in some extraordinary way within a human person, had the power necessary to overcome the hostile cosmic forces that produced feelings of helplessness and powerlessness—lack of security—within individuals. The experience of salvation, therefore, is described as an experience whereby the saved participates in the power of the divine. This participation perhaps indicates the essential difference between redemption and salvation: In the paradigm of redemption, one experiences the power of the divine; whereas in that of salvation, one's existence is transformed from the powerless to the powerful by partaking of the divinity.

The consequences of these experiences are striking, particularly if they are viewed in terms of relationships of power. The language of salvation belongs, first and foremost, to the discourse of power. Like all descriptions of experience, the metaphorical language that is used to describe salvation and redemption ultimately derives from readily available social realities, which necessarily involve significations and constructions of power that inevitably include expressions of gender.[2] Metaphors descriptive of saving will thus be expected to derive from experiences of power in the social world. Those who have power in a society, especially the ability to generate or control symbols, will therefore be the primary providers and guardians of images of power in religious discourse. When the powerless in society appear as figures of power in that discourse, this appearance may be viewed as an extraordinary situation or even a cosmic reversal.

In both the paradigm of redemption and that of salvation, the power of an agent is effective on behalf of a recipient. The achievement of a position of security, state of health, or state of being rescued or restored is not that of the saved except insofar as they are the *receivers* of actions by a powerful patron, deity, or patron deity. In the redemption history of Israel, YHWH's act of redemption of the people of Israel is the powerful act of one mighty lord versus another, the pharaoh (among the other gods) of Egypt. YHWH is able to rescue "his" people from an illegitimate and alien possessor, whether he actually "owns" them or is related to them as the "redeemer" (*go'el*), the "next of kin" obliged to rescue his "own" family from the power of another. In many of the Greco-Roman mystery religions, the saved achieve salvation by participation in or sharing of the *power* of a mighty deity, especially power over death. Indeed, as Luther H. Martin has observed, "The Greek title 'savior' . . . designated extraordinary personalities, divine or human, who were active in world affairs and were considered to have transformed a situation for the better."[3] In both cases, the experience of being redeemed or saved is to have power operating on one's behalf, and in some cases to become empowered. Let us now examine these two paradigms in more historical and semantic detail.

The Paradigm of Redemption

The important work on the contextualization of Hebrew words for salvation, John F. A. Sawyer's *Semantics in Biblical Research* (1972), which builds on James Barr's *Semantics of Biblical Language* (1961), emphasizes the fact that not only must "an adequate definition of context precede every statement," but also that the "original" context of a term may not be the most important.[4] The "meaning" of terms, therefore, cannot be divorced from the meaning that they have to the speaker(s) and hearer(s) in a particular social and historical situation or situations. Carrying Sawyer's contention a bit farther, we could say that the prevalent meanings of words or metaphors over time dominate and overshadow the original meanings, in a way similar to the way we are trained to interpret visual images, a way that is historically and culturally conditioned, so that we cannot imagine either reading or seeing in any other ways.

One of the ways in which semantic studies of the Bible are further complicated is the translation of Hebrew terms (and their attendant contexts) into Greek terms and their attendant contexts, and since the Septuagint (LXX), the translation into Greek of the Hebrew texts, was the most influential translation in the spread of early Christian communities, the problem is an important one. Thus, we may find that the Greek term *sozo* (save) is used without very much differentiation in the LXX between the "original" meanings of redemption as "ransom" or "buying out" (*g'l; pdh*)—that is, the transference of the ownership of a person from an "alien" owner to the "proper" owner or to the next of kin—and the allied term *ysh*[e] (deliver), whose hiphil form, *hoshia'*, usually is understood as causing "rescue," "enlargement," or "liberation."[5] The "original" understandings of these terms and their cognates may have been much different, but the use of these terms over time tends to collapse such distinctions, which may nevertheless serve as devices for exploration of meanings.

Terms for redemption in scripture typically imply a transfer of status of the individual or a people. In traditional Jewish thought, YHWH is the deity who is the proper "owner" or "next of kin" (*go'el*) of the people of Israel. The two terms used in the Tanak to express this relationship were originally derived from the language of legal possession of living things (*pdh*) and from family law (*g'l*).[6] The root *pdh* is associated with the "redemption" ("buying back" or paying a fine) of the life of the person killed by the "ox that gores" (Ex. 21:30); the "redemption" of a daughter who does not please her new "master" after being sold by her father into slavery (Ex. 21:7–8); or the "redemption" of the Israelite firstborn (all of whom "belong" to YHWH) through the dedication (= sacrifice) of the Levites to YHWH (Num. 8:15–16).

In the realm of family/property law, the root *g'l* is applied to "the action of the next of kin to recover forfeited property of a kinsman or to purchase his freedom if he has fallen into slavery."[7] The next of kin, or *go'el,* is the "redeemer" of the property of a kinsman sold into debt-slavery and of the life of a kinsman by taking in exchange the life of his murderer (Num. 35:19).[8] The responsibilities of the *go'el* with regard to his kin, including the obligation to redeem the future of a kinsman's family by marrying his childless widow, are part of the tantalizing plot of the folktale of Ruth and Naomi (e.g., Ruth 4:4–6). In an extension of this concept, YHWH becomes the personal *go'el* of Job, his vindicator before judgment (*go'eliy* [Job 19:25]). In the writings of Second Isaiah (Isa. 40–55) particularly, YHWH is the *go'el* of Israel.[9]

Thus the redemptive relationship between Israel and Israel's God, who acts on its behalf as its rightful "owner" (e.g., Ex. 13:1; Num. 8:15–16) or as its "next of (male) kin," is modeled upon the available social and familial relationships of the person of power (master, father, male head of clan) who acts in such a way that the status of those without power is changed from the worse to the better. Actually, the experience of redemption is spoken of less in terms of change than in terms of restoration: restoration to the proper owner or previous state of the relationship, a relationship that is the expression of a dynamic of power. Hence, a person or a people is redeemed from a situation of alienation in its root sense, "belonging to another." As the agent of redemption, YHWH, the God of Israel, is envisioned as its redeemer from the situation of slavery, and also, in later prophetic language, as its redeemer from the exile in Babylon—both situations of alienation of a people from its rightful owner. The obligation of the next of kin in Israelite law to redeem the forfeited property of near kin, or to purchase their freedom once enslaved, provides the metaphor for YHWH as the agent who achieves Israel's freedom by paying the price of ransom.[10] Moreover, during the exile, in the second temple period, whenever Israel as a nation was dominated by a foreign power—be it Babylonia, Syria, or Rome—its theologians, seeking an answer to this problem of the apparent failure of God's justice, found it for the most part in the responsibility, individually and collectively, of the people of Israel to their redeeming God. Once again, the paradigm for the relationship of Israel to YHWH was the situation of the Israelites in Egypt—estrangement and enslavement under a foreign and therefore illegitimate power.

There is another element of the redemptive relationship, however, one derived also from law and involving penalty and payment. As Shaye Cohen notes of the concept of redemption in the second temple period, "Human courts do not accept repentance. A criminal must pay a penalty for his or her crime."[11] This metaphor, derived from the forensic understanding of redemption, is applied to YHWH, the God of Israel, who as both righteous judge and source of justice at once demands and pays Israel's penalty. The idea of paying a penalty is thus associated with the idea of redemption: A debt must be cancelled, a crime must be expiated, a price must be paid. Thus, the concept of redemption implies a defect that must be remedied, a fault for which restitution must be made. In the redemption history of Israel, every time Israel became alienated from its God, usually through apostasy, its life or existence metaphorically became forfeit. This dynamic is formulaically expressed in the book of Judges, in which the apostasy of the tribes to YHWH is punished by alienation, even by YHWH's "selling" his people into the hands of another owner (Judg. 2:14).

During the exile, the idea of retributive punishment as a price that is paid for sin is a prominent idea in the writings of Second Isaiah:

> Speak tenderly to Jerusalem
>   and cry to her,
> that she has served her term,
>   that her penalty is paid;
> she has received from YHWH's hand
>   double for all her sins.
>   (Isa. 40:2, NRSV, modified)

Second Isaiah also develops the idea of the redemptive and vicarious suffering of the righteous servant of God. In the so-called Servant Song of Isaiah 53, so important for the development of later Christology as a means of explaining the death of Jesus the messiah, the *'ebed YHWH,* the servant of God, bears "the sin of many" (Isa. 53:12). The idea of redemptive suffering on behalf of the apostasy of the people is also developed in 2 Maccabees, where both Eleazar and the mother and her seven sons die faithful to the laws of YHWH in the midst of the infidelity of the rest. The last of the seven to die expresses this concept: "With me and my brothers may the Almighty's anger, which has justly fallen on all our race, be ended" (2 Macc. 7:38, NEB). In the New Testament, the writings of Paul in particular express the Christian interpretation of the dynamic of sin and alienation through the atonement of Christ as a "ransom" (*apolytrosis*) from the alien power of sin (Rom. 3:21–26).[12]

Another model of the need for and experience of redemption is derived from a different source: the metaphor of marriage and marital infidelity. In the preexilic period, the northern prophet Hosea (ca. 786–746 B.C.E.) had expressed the idea of apostasy metaphorically as the infidelity of the bride Israel toward her husband, YHWH:

> She is not my wife,
> and I am not her husband—
> [Let her] put away her whoring from her face,
> and her adultery from between her breasts.
>   (Hos. 2:2, NRSV, modified)

The relationship between YHWH and Israel is now envisioned as a covenant between husband and wife, expressing the intimate relationship of "knowledge" (knowing, as well as intercourse) between Israel (the wife) and YHWH (the husband). Just as the literal relationship between wife and husband in Israelite society could be strained and broken by the wife's adultery, in which case the wife's life became forfeit, along with that of her lover (see Lev. 20:10–11; Deut. 22:22), so the covenantal relationship between YHWH and Israel, metaphorically expressed by Hosea as that of faithful husband and faithless wife, could also be broken. But in the latter case, although the wife's (Israel's) life could be forfeit, YHWH does not accept the forfeiture, but redeems his faithless wife from the lovers who illegitimately possessed her. The wife (Israel) is then restored to her husband (YHWH). As Hosea expresses it, YHWH "speaks tenderly" or "speaks to the heart" of Israel and wins her back. She then "knows" him as he knows her: The relationship of intimate knowledge is restored (Hos. 2:14–20). Hosea's portrayal of the redemption of the wife (Israel) by the husband (YHWH) is thus an idealization of an aspect of the actual relationship between husband and wife. When Israel is restored to YHWH, moreover, a new and better relationship obtains: YHWH is no longer to be addressed as *ba'al* or "master" (owner), but as *'ish* or "husband" (Hos. 2:16).

This idealized situation may be contrasted to a similar incident and similar relationship, but one with a very different outcome. The incident is described in Judges 19 and is linked to the language of "winning back" the wife/Israel. In this story, meant to illustrate the criminality of the Benjaminites and support the historian's judgment that Israel needs a king, the concubine of a Levite (both are unnamed) returns to her father's house. In the Greek and Old Latin versions of the text, she did so because she "became angry" with the Levite; in the Hebrew Masoretic and Syriac texts, she "played the harlot," like Hosea's metaphorical Israel. In either case, she deserts her owner who "took her for himself." The Levite goes to "speak to her heart" as YHWH speaks to the heart of Israel in Hosea. While the Levite actually owns her (as is demonstrated in the horrible end to the story, in which he allows her to be gang-raped to death in his own stead), he initially does not insist on his ownership, but rather pleads for the voluntary return of his "wife" to him. In the denouement of the story, the torn body of the woman, cut into twelve pieces, symbolizes the torn body of Israel.[13] In both of these texts, a woman's body is used as a metaphor for Israel. In Hosea's prophecy, the "illegitimate" exercise of female sexuality outside of marriage symbolizes the apostasy of Israel; in the Judges 19 narrative, the female body, which does not "belong" to the woman herself, but to those who possess her, is the symbol of the perfidy and lawlessness of male Israelites. In both cases, the female body is connected with sexual transgression and stands as a metaphor for infidelity.

Certainly the metaphor of adultery or harlotry for the behavior of Israel toward YHWH is only one among many, but the analogy of religious apostasy to female sexual transgression continued to serve as a dominant metaphor in male prophets' and theologians' descriptive language of the relationship of Israel to its God. In their view, all Israelites needed to be redeemed from the alienation from YHWH brought about either by captivity or apostasy. When Israel was visualized as female, however, the alienation she needed to be redeemed from was brought about by her own adultery and prostitution, states that were visualized as a transfer of ownership of her body. Thus female "fault" became localized in the "illegitimate" exercise of women's sexuality. The seduction and seductivity of the human female continue to be used in other contexts as male-developed metaphors suggesting fidelity to YHWH or its opposite. In Proverbs, the "adulteress" or "strange (foreign) woman" (*'ishsha' zara'*), against whom various instructors continually warn young men, is also a metaphor for Folly, who seduces young men away from Wisdom (see Prov. 9). If therefore the infidel Israel is symbolized by the unfaithful woman, her redeemer is symbolized by the male YHWH: The language and its division of gender are metaphorically carried over to the divine being because that being is also given a personality. As Rita M. Gross has noted, "The metaphor of a gender-free person is impossible. Persons are male or female."[14] Moreover, the use of the metaphor of infidelity to describe disobedience and apostasy tended to limit the concept of sin to sexuality, and particularly to female sexuality. This connection later became explicit in interpretations of Eve as a symbol in intertestamental Judaism and formative Christianity, and in interpretations of the Fall in the latter: Female physicality and "unruly" sexuality, always turning away from its "proper" orientation, can thus be made to oppose male rationality and spirituality, which must not allow the threatening power of female sexuality to get out of control. The apocryphal book of Jesus ben Sirach, for example, can praise a female persona, Wisdom, as the maternal teacher of the young (Sir. 4:11–19), but at the same time assign to woman as a whole the responsibility for sin and death: "From a woman sin had its beginning, and because of her we all die" (Sir. 25:24, NRSV). The female nature, identified in such texts specifically with the physical and even more with the sexual, is depicted in some sense as fundamentally defective and in need of redemption.[15] If therefore the female needs redemption to a larger degree than the male, the agent of redemption, by this logic, cannot be female unless, as in the case of Gnostic Sophia, she redeems herself first, or, as in the case of Mary, she is herself first redeemed by the power of the male deity from the taint of sin: that is, from the taint of the exercise of her sexuality.

There are some models in biblical Judaism, apart from that of Wisdom, in which the redeemer is envisioned as a woman or a woman acts as redeemer. These will be discussed later in connection with salvation. There are not many of these; they are not dominant models; and they, too, are idealizations embedded in largely androcentric texts. In these texts the role of woman as redeemer is usually limited to the function of childbirth, an acceptable function of female sexuality. In the same context in which Hosea speaks of the relationship of Israel and YHWH in the exodus as being one of child to parent, he also likens YHWH to a mother or nurse who draws the infant Ephraim with the "leading strings" of (maternal) love out of Egypt and through the wilderness (Hos. 11:3–4). The mother's love thus redeems the kidnapped child. In the story of Ruth and Naomi, it is Boaz—the male kinsman, the *go'el*—who takes over the part of the redeemer, both to redeem Naomi's land and to raise up children to her dead son by the latter's widow, Ruth; however, it is Ruth who is spoken of as performing the redemptive act by giving birth to Naomi's "son," and Naomi by her counsel makes possible the redemption of the fortunes of her line. Indeed, at the birth of Ruth's son, Obed, the women of Bethlehem bless Naomi because of the birth of her *go'el* from the one who means "more than seven sons," her daughter-in-law Ruth (Ruth 4:14–17). Although there are other examples of women who act powerfully or through the power of YHWH to restore the fortunes of their families or of Israel, the language used with regard to these women belongs more to the paradigm of salvation than redemption strictly speaking, and to this language we now turn.

The Paradigm of Salvation

According to Sawyer's semantic definitions of words for salvation in biblical Hebrew, these convey the general idea of "deliverance," "rescue," and "help."[16] The most frequent of these, *hoshia'*, is used 95 percent of the time in "religious contexts," that is, contexts that have YHWH "or an Israelite leader appointed by him" as the subject of the verb.[17] All of the seven other verbs for salvation occur in contexts of religious, forensic, or other situations of deliverance, where aid comes from an outside power.

Another biblical semanticist, James Barr, has pointed out that while there is little in the *frequency* of words denoting a concentration on the idea of salvation in the Hebrew Bible, "Themes and images may speak of salvation even when the obvious surface terminology is lacking."[18] In Barr's opinion, more characteristic of the language of salvation in the Pentateuch are phrases of agency, such as "[YHWH] brought them out...." In the historical books, the term *hoshia'* refers mainly to military victories, with the judges in particular seen as being "raised up" by YHWH as individual instances of a *moshia'*, deliverer or savior. In the prophetic and later apocalyptic writings, hopes for salvation have gained an "articulated picture" of what they seek deliverance from, primarily hostile and oppressive powers of the earth.[19]

Barr's semantic and contextual analysis of the metaphorical language of salvation in the Hebrew Bible is impressive, not the least because of three issues he raises: first, that salvation comes through *agency*, whether divine or empowered by the deity; second (although he does not directly state this), that salvation, especially in the later literature of the biblical period, implies rescue from a hostile power, whether human or cosmic; and third, that salvation is related to redemption in that "deliverances in the Pentateuch do not alter the relationship between the men and their God; . . . they confirm and re-establish the relationship already existing."[20]

Before attempting to analyze the third conclusion and its ramifications for women and their salvation, we should first point out how closely these Hebrew terms and their contexts parallel Greco-Roman understandings of salvation. In Greek and Roman literature from Homer to Dio Chrysostom, salvation language is used to describe an "acutely dynamic act," one that achieves the rescue of a person or persons from war and other calamities, judicial condemnation, illness, and "all the perils of life."[21] Thus we might speak of salvation (*soteria* in Greek, *salus* in Latin) according to its root meaning of "health, safety, security." The German word for salvation as well as health, *Heil,* if stripped of its theological freight, perhaps best conveys the sense of the Greek. The language of salvation might also, like related terms in Hebrew that the Greek verb *sozo* translates in the Septuagint, convey a sense of restoration to a former state from a state of calamity. This restoration is effected through the power of a deity or other "powerful personality," even through a human person who is endowed with power by a divine one. We might also understand salvation, especially in the Hellenistic world, in the same way as Martin describes it, "meaning transformation," either a transformation of the existing (bad) situation to a former (good) situation or of the existing situation into a better or ideal one.[22]

What is most important for our purposes, however, is the way the *agent* of salvation effects this transformation. Whether understood in its Judaic, Greek, or Roman context, the experience of salvation necessarily involves power, a power that is bestowed by the one who has it. In all three contexts, the one who is responsible for deliverance from danger and restoration to safety is always a *personal* agent.[23] In the case of the judges of Israel, the

judge as *moshia'* or deliverer is "raised up" by YHWH in
order to perform an action of rescue similar to that of
YHWH himself. The nominative *moshia'* is in fact used
almost exclusively for YHWH in the Hebrew canon, except for three times in denoting such "judges" (Judg. 3:9,
15; Neh. 9:27).[24] These persons appear to be, but are
not always, primarily warriors. Indeed, as Barr asserts,
the "deliverer" (*moshia'*) may perform an act of rescue
(as in the case of Ehud [Judg. 3:15–30]) that is an act
of subterfuge, rather than an act on the battlefield.[25] In
just such a way does Jael, through subterfuge, become
the agent of YHWH's deliverance of Israel, rather than
the warrior of the battle at Mt. Tabor, Barak. In addition, the latter requires the assistance of another female
agent of YHWH, the judge Deborah. The Song of Deborah in Judges 5 praises Jael for her craft in the execution
of the enemy general, Sisera, calling her "most blessed
of women" and, by implication, the "friend" of YHWH.
In the apocryphal book of Judith, the heroine, whose behavior is obviously modeled on the craft of Jael, manages
to deliver her people from an alien power, acting with
the "power" of God (Judith 13:19). George W. Nickelsburg observes that not only does the story of Judith have
a "parabolic quality" in recapitulating Israel's redemptive
history, but the figure of Judith herself is a "personification" of many Israelite heroines: Miriam, Deborah, Jael,
and the wise women of Thebez (Judg. 9:53–54) and Abel
(2 Sam. 20:14–22).[26]

Craftiness, subterfuge, and even subversion are indeed
elements of the aspect of practical wisdom valued as clev-
erness in many ancient Mediterranean societies. While
craft is employed by the hero (e.g., Jacob, Odysseus)
when he is temporarily disadvantaged or deprived of
control in a situation, craft as a less direct form of gain-
ing one's end is particular to women, who are normally
excluded "from the established hierarchies of authority
and power in a society," as Claudia V. Camp observes.[27]
It may also express an aspect of Wisdom of a lower

sort: that is, the aspect of practical behavior that is potentially accessible to all.[28] In biblical Judaism, subterfuge is an acceptable means of action for heroines if it is used for a good cause. Tamar uses it to force her father-in-law, Judah, to perform his duty as next of kin; and it is employed in a good cause by Ruth, Naomi, Esther, and Judith, a Hellenistic Jewish heroine. These women procure not only the redemption of their own houses and family lines (Tamar, Ruth, Naomi), but also the salvation of their people (Esther, Judith). In the canonical book of Proverbs and in the apocryphal books of Sirach and the Wisdom of Solomon, the salvific role of personified Wisdom is, as Camp convincingly argues, modeled upon these women. Although idealized by the males who are writing the androcentric literature in which they appear, these figures—because they are metaphorical images—may nevertheless be grounded in both "the idea and experience of 'woman' in ancient Israel."[29]

While indirect means may be the only ones women could employ in the patriarchal society of ancient Israel, as in other patriarchal societies, they are nevertheless seen, even by the male biblical writers, as achieving divine ends, and further as representing or even embodying the dynamic actions of YHWH. In the case of the book of Judith, for example, as Toni Craven has observed in her rhetorical-critical analysis, the first seven chapters of the book are devoted to describing "communities in which men play all the leading roles" and which are characterized by domination by the strong and intimidation of the powerless.[30] Judith's heroic action may thus be regarded as the assertion of the power of YHWH through one disregarded by the ordinary or normal channels of authority. The rhetoric of Judith itself emphasizes the dynamic of reversal by stressing the fact that YHWH has triumphed through the "hand of a female" (*theleia*).[31] Mary's Song in Luke 1:46–55 echoes this dynamic of reversal as envisioned by the early Christian eschatological communities: God's paradoxical triumph through the agency of the normally powerless.

The actions of these women who partake of divine power, together with the saving advice and counsel of wise women and prophetesses who contribute to the image of divine Wisdom in Judaism, will be discussed in more detail in the chapter on Wisdom. For the present, it is sufficient to note that, even in the largely patriarchal history of ancient Israel, the actions of women might be seen as salvific and could provide, however shadowy and indistinct, a possible model for a type of savior. However, the observation of Martin about the "flirtation" of Judaism with a female personification of the divine, Hokhmah/Sophia, should serve as a caution: "By the second century C.E., . . . Judaism was clearly reestablished as the patriarchal Judaism of the rabbis and retained little trace of its flirt with the feminine."[32] This judgment is also true of patriarchal Christianity. To use one example, Clement of Rome's praise of Judith, typical of his age and milieu (first century C.E.), holds her up as an example of a woman who exhibited "manly valor" (i.e., *virtus;* Greek *andreia*) (*1 Clem.* 55.45).[33] The idealization of a woman is achieved because she conforms to a male ideal.

One of the powerful agents of God in the late second temple period in Judaism is the *mashiah* (Greek *christos*). However variously interpreted, this "anointed one"— king, priest, or prophet—is definitely an ideal *male* figure. Moreover, as William Scott Green has pointed out, the term as used in the Hebrew Bible denotes "one invested, usually by God, with power and leadership," although not necessarily an eschatological figure. Throughout the postexilic history of Israel, the anointed one was primarily envisioned as a king, one of the Davidic line who would free Israel (e.g., Luke 24:21), but there were conflicting ideas of God's anointed agent, the only unifying trait among them being that this agent was "raised up" by the divine power as the judges and other types of *moshia'* had been.[34] When the followers of Jesus' "restoration movement" sought to find a locus within Judaism for the preacher of the coming kingdom of God that had apparently failed to come, and a justification and interpretation for his death, the choice of the title *mashiah* (*christos*) as the preferred one for Jesus "gave the figure of the messiah a diachronic dimension."[35] In short, the messiah as God's agent of a *future* restoration became much more important for Christians than it had ever been for other Jews who were their contemporaries.

Nevertheless, although the term is used by Paul almost always as a title for Jesus, it is in Paul's letters that Jesus as the Christ, the messiah of Jewish restoration theology, was translated into Christ as the cosmic savior. In this context, Hyam Maccoby notes, "The basic theme in the Pauline myth [of Jesus] can be summed up in one phrase: the descent of the divine saviour."[36] While Maccoby is probably in error about the provenance of this mythic figure (he locates it in Gnosticism), he is nonetheless correct in the assumption that for Paul, Jesus took on the configuration of a figure that was recognizable both from its appearance in Jewish Wisdom, especially of the Hellenistic period, and in Greco-Roman religions. This figure is best articulated in the early Christian hymn quoted by Paul in Philippians 2:6–11, which summarizes the role of the cosmic savior:

> Who, though he was in the form of God,
>   did not regard equality with God
>   as something to be exploited,
> but emptied himself,
>   taking the form of a slave,
>   being born in human likeness....
> Therefore God also highly exalted him
>   and gave him the name
>   that is above every name.
>   (Phil. 2:6–7, 9, NRSV)

Charles H. Talbert observes that the idea of divine figures appearing in human shape was an old one in
Greek and Roman mythology and "could be used by
Greco-Roman authors to interpret the lives of historical figures."[37] To Hellenistic Gentile audiences, then, the
idea of a descending-ascending savior would not be as
unfamiliar as that of a predicted Jewish king. But Judaism itself had developed an understanding of Wisdom
that incorporated elements of Greco-Roman mythology,
at least in its adoption of a descending-ascending divine figure, as delineated particularly in Ben Sirach (24),
Wisdom of Solomon (9–10), and the pseudepigraphical
1 Enoch (42:1–2).[38] However, as will be shown later in the
chapter on Wisdom as a savior figure, although the literary hypostasis of Wisdom is female, the incarnation of
Wisdom is not. Even in the Hellenistic period and especially in the early centuries of formative Judaism, she is
increasingly seen as incarnated in *male* sages, those who
study Torah. As Jacob Neusner observes, "Among the
available models for the incarnation of God [in formative
Judaism] the one that predominated entailed representation of God as sage."[39] Identification of Wisdom as male
rather than female was assisted in Hellenistic Judaism
by writers like Philo, who also used messianic terminology as "the allegorical designator for the *Logos*."[40] The
evangelist John, a Hellenistic Jewish Christian, also saw
the descending-ascending savior as the male personage
of the Logos, who is incarnated in the male person of
Jesus of Nazareth. Paul himself spoke of Christ as in-
carnating both "the wisdom (*sophia*) and power of God"
(1 Cor. 1:24). If Wisdom had been strongly identified
as female in Jewish theology, it would have been less
easy for the Christian Paul to use this grammatically
feminine term for the male Christ. In depersonalizing
Wisdom as female—that is, making the gender of the
noun have no relevance to the person of the figure—Paul
and other Christians were able to repersonalize Wisdom
as male.

But if the intersection of the Jewish Wisdom tradition with Greco-Roman piety provided—as Martin correctly asserts—a strong inclusion of the female, later to be strenuously redefined so as to *exclude* her, where was the female represented as a salvific figure in Gentile Hellenism? In order to answer this question, it is necessary first to remember that Gentile Hellenism (or, to use a more correct term, Greco-Roman religiosity), however it might appear in some aspects as syncretistic or even monotheistic, was essentially either polytheistic or monistic, the latter being the tendency in philosophical religiosity. It thus follows that the Greeks and then the Romans perceived their cosmos as being inhabited by various powers who could effect the restoration or transformation they regarded as salvation.

The traditional Greek view of salvation (*soteria*) included both the concepts of keeping things (especially the "ship of state," the polis) on an even keel in the interests of the dominant party and restoring them to their former state after a period of upheaval. Perhaps this traditional concept may best be summarized by the tragic poet worshiped by the polis of Athens after his death, Sophocles. In his *Antigone,* the ancient Greek city of Thebes has just been restored after a destructive civil war led by the feuding sons of Oedipus. Creon, as restored king of Thebes, envisions the city itself as a savior, providing the safety and security of each individual in it:

Nor could I count the enemy of the land [i.e., city]
friend to myself, not I who know so well
that it is she who saves us, sailing straight,
and only so can we have friends at all.
(*Antigone* 187–90)[41]

Because traditional Greek thought saw divinity as a fluid concept, as a force or dynamic power, a power perceived as being divine might be anything or anyone that could achieve rescue or personal or public preservation (i.e., "safety") from perils as varied as those of war (e.g., Homer, *Iliad* 15.292ff.; Plato, *Symposium* 220D; Aelius Aristides, *Orations* 45.13), shipwreck (Homer, *Odyssey* 5.130), judicial condemnation (Xenophon, *Greek History* 5.4.26), or illness.[42]

In the Hellenistic period, generally understood as embracing the history of the Greek-influenced Mediterranean area from the fourth to the late first century B.C.E., the expressions of power in Greek thought, religion, and literature were enlarged. Just as the old polis system became incorporated into larger sociopolitical units, like kingdoms (*basileiai*), so also the traditional deities took on larger spheres of power, particularly those spheres of control associated with planets or stars. One of the greatest powers of the Hellenistic world reflected the chaos in self-orientation that was caused by the turmoil of the period. First grammatically, then metaphorically female, she was Tyche or Fortuna, Chance or Fortune, whose caprice initially reflected the fluctuations of status and power within the Hellenistic world, but who became identified by male authors with feminine caprice and fickleness. One of the reasons that Isis became such a powerful savior goddess was that her power was seen as being capable of successfully opposing and conquering the power of Tyche[43] and of an equally powerful and equally binding, if not as capricious, force—*Heimarmene* ("Constraint" or "Limit"), envisioned by the Stoics as having the power of Fate. From the earlier, more confident Stoicism, in which Heimarmene gave persons the ability to assent to "the impressions presented to the mind" or equally to reject them, the more pessimistic Stoicism of the second century and later came closer to the popular perspective, giving the concept a more prominent and more sinister cosmic role, one that was closer to the idea of fortune or chance.[44]

The Romans—like the Greeks, whose literature and philosophy the Romans appropriated and, through syncretism, made uniquely their own—traditionally viewed the world as divided into realms of divine influence, or numina, which were not originally personified. Places, objects, and persons could all have a numen, but the term above all signified power, one that presided over terrestrial, human, and cosmic affairs, and one that needed to be placated and sometimes compelled to act through human supplication. Although for the Romans, as for the Greeks, there were many degrees and spheres of power, the most powerful numina had the widest spheres of influence and were both the most to be feared and therefore also the most to be supplicated. In terms of traditional public piety, this meant a formal system of reverencing power—from that of Jupiter (the traditional head of the Olympian family and "ruler of gods and humans"), to that of other Olympians and the earthly political systems of power they supported, to that of the head of the household, *familia,* or other associated group, who was usually male. For most of the periods of Roman history with which we are concerned, "paternal power" (*patria potestas*), the authority of the head of the *familia* over it, was that of life and death, however rarely exercised it may have been.

Since people in the Hellenistic and Greco-Roman worlds tended to see the cosmos as a series of interlocking and even concentric spheres of power and control, they developed means of addressing the powers on a variety of levels, from the elaborate system of public ritual (Greek *eusebeia;* Latin *pietas*) to that more common and personal ritual called by the intellectuals *superstitio.* The evidence of the vast collection of magical papyri (magical spells and formula written on papyrus) from Greco-Roman Egypt shows that, from the top of the social and political hierarchy to its bottom, men and women were concerned about the operation of various cosmic powers and their manipulation. As Martin again succinctly observes, "The ...conventions of folk piety belonged, therefore, to the same world as the so-called 'higher' forms of spirituality and knowledge."[45]

In this system of belief, an agent of salvation needed to be or to have a power equal to that of the oppressive cosmic forces. This savior, as C. J. Bleeker has observed, had three aspects: first, a combination of human and divine characteristics, as in a king, hero, sage, or prophet; second, the ability to mediate between the divine and human realms; third, and perhaps foremost, a "dynamic (active) personality," the personality of one who "cares for the well-being [of humans]."[46] Within the Greco-Roman world, a savior or *soter* therefore was a *personal* agent.[47] Because of the powers believed to reside within the cosmic sphere, this personal agent, in order to effect salvation on earth, had either to be in communion with these powers (as a mediator), to share in these powers (usually through divine birth or commission), or to equal them (as in the hero cults or Hellenistic ruler cults). The title *soter* was first applied to deities as rescuers, preservers, and sustainers of life, and especially as patron deities of cities. Those deities who were foremost in power, Zeus for example, were those earliest connected with salvation: One of Zeus's most common epithets was *Soter*, and to him as such the third cup of wine was poured at banquets.[48] Among humans, the title began to be applied by suppliants to their helper in distress (e.g., Aeschylus, *Suppliants* 980–82; Sophocles, *Oedipus the King* 302–4), and then, by extension, especially in the Hellenistic and early imperial periods, to others, particularly statesmen and rulers, but even to physicians and philosophers.[49] Therefore the power of the heavenly realm was seen as located and embodied in particular human figures, whose saving power was manifested, often through the performance of miraculous acts, on behalf of those without power.[50] This figure is the model for one aspect of Jesus in the New Testament, the *theios aner*, the "divine man"; this expression of Jesus Christ as the powerful Son of God was especially effective in hellenized contexts. The power of the deity has come down to earth and resides in a human being whose miracles serve as evidence of that divine power and its incarnation.[51]

Yet there is another aspect of the savior in the Greco-Roman world, one that is connected with the power that confers or bestows benefit, usually on a group of people. This aspect is designated by the epithet *euergetes*, "benefactor/benefactress," another title that was a favorite one for Zeus in ancient Greece, and was later applied to rulers, statesmen, and officials. Ptolemy I Soter, the Greek ruler of Egypt, was addressed as *euergetes* because of his virtue (*arete*) while he was addressed as *soter* because of his deeds.[52] According to Martin Nilsson, Greek popular religion had always had its own deified humans in the form of heroes. Hero cults had grown up around the tombs of eponymous ancestors and other persons, including benefactors, believed to have preternatural powers. As Moses Hadas and Morton Smith note, these powers continued to have an influence after death: "Originally, in its technical sense, the word [*hero*] meant little more than ghost, and the offerings made at a *heroon* [hero's tomb or shrine] were intended to ward off the harmful interference with the living of which the ghost might be capable."[53] Later, the hero cults were intended to "assert [the heroes'] potency and to evoke their aid or inspiration in the field of their own achievement."[54] Even the tragic poet Sophocles, because of his piety and his benefits to the city of Athens, was the recipient of a hero cult after his death: "They say that the Athenians, in their desire to do honor to Sophocles after his death, built a hero's shrine to him and called him Dexion, 'he that receives,' for his reception of Asclepius."[55]

Such cults in the Hellenistic and Greco-Roman periods continued to be established to commemorate benefits conferred by persons who exercised their powers on behalf of their cities and demes.[56] Around the *heroon* of the benefactor, as around the tomb of the medieval saint, miracles—actually, the continuing of the person's benefits—might be expected to occur. Plutarch relates one such instance regarding Cleomenes of Sparta (third century B.C.E.), who killed himself in a failed attempt to liberate the Egyptians from the Ptolemies. His corpse, flayed and crucified, was the site of a miraculous manifestation: A "great serpent" coiled around it to protect it from predatory birds. Accordingly, says Plutarch, "awe and fear" were engendered in the populace, causing women to perform purification rituals, "for the man who had been taken away had been beloved of the gods and preternaturally endowed. The Alexandrians visited the site frequently to worship."[57] While this popular aspect of belief was consistently scoffed at by the philosophers, especially the Stoics, it was nevertheless the Stoic perception of a certain "divine power" (*vis divina; theia dyamis*) that facilitated the connection between that power and human activity. This divine power, often viewed as the equivalent of the Logos or divine reason, was seen as pervading the universe and making communication between divine and human realms possible.[58] Cicero, for example, notes that while the "vulgar superstition" believes that gods exist in human shape, many useful things are called by the names of gods, and humans are deified for their benefits to others (*On the Nature of the Gods* 2.26.62). He also notes that "already in Greece, they hold that many deities have been made from human beings," and that, even in Rome, following the "deification" of Julius Caesar, "there are those who are thought to have been recently enrolled and received into heaven" (3.15.39). The Christian writer Theodoretus criticized this tendency on the part of the Greeks: "Afterwards they deified those who had done anything well, or had demonstrated bravery in battle, or began some kind of agriculture, or provided a wine for anybody, and even constructed temples for them" (*On the Curing of Greek Affections* 3.24–28).[59]

With this type of model for the savior, where would one expect women to fit in? In the realm of female deities, those goddesses who saved or protected cities by their power might be expected to be prominent. This is certainly the case with the goddess Athena, protectress of Athens. Athena saves her city in a way that is typical of patron deities: She is a warrior goddess and a virgin, transformed from her earlier incarnation as a mother goddess. The attributes of Athena, as with other Greek goddesses, indicate, in idealized form, what was valued by those who were dominant in the society: that is, males. As Mary R. Lefkowitz has pointed out, while we do not know very much about ancient women's reactions to myths, and possess still less of those women's writing, we can say that ancient "myths place emphasis on the kind of experiences and problems— although in idealized or exaggerated form—that most ancient women would encounter in the course of their lives."[60] While in myth there were two models of women's existence—virginity and "involvement with males"—only one of these, involvement with males, was actually available to real women, since, for most of Greek as well as Roman women, virginity was seen as a temporary state prior to marriage.[61] Virgin goddesses like Athena and Artemis, "killer of women," had power, like that of males, to maintain their virginity. Athena in fact wears the accoutrements of a (male) warrior as the protectress of her city—the helmet, spear, breastplate (*aegis*) with the terrifying Gorgon's head, and the shield. Artemis also has weaponry: the bow and arrows that she has in common with her male twin, Apollo. The fact that Athena is a virgin also annuls her threatening female sexuality, which is controlled and ultimately annihilated, as symbolized by the head of Medusa on her *aegis*. As Rosemary R. Ruether has pointed out, "The most dignified female figures in Greek mythology were virgins, separated from threatening female sexual power."[62]

Such power threatened the men who controlled the cities just as they controlled the women who belonged to them. This may be demonstrated by the contrast of Athena with another patroness of a city: Aphrodite, the goddess of Corinth. Aphrodite, the symbol of the power of female sexuality, was an example of marital infidelity from the time of Homer (*Odyssey* 8.300–365). Her temple in Corinth was also said, perhaps libelously and certainly disapprovingly, to have had one thousand cultic prostitutes in the period before 146 B.C.E., when the Romans destroyed the city. Her unsavory reputation, which was widely bestowed upon her city, went into the Greek vocabulary as a verb, *korinthazomai,* "to fornicate." Certainly Aphrodite, while perceived as having power, possessed that female power ancient males, at least from the evidence of their writing, found so disruptive, the power of female sexuality. They could not conceive of such power as being salvific.

In ancient Greece, as in ancient Rome, with some exceptions, the best divine models *for women* were primarily deities related to the control of their reproductive capacities.[63] These models were usually created by men in their idealized image of women, exhibiting the values of the dominant groups in society, which in ancient Mediterranean societies, without exception, were male. Therefore, as Eva Cantarella has observed, even a dominant female deity cannot "be considered proof of woman's social and political power. The most that can be assumed is that this is a sign of the dignity that society ascribed to the maternal function."[64] Although there were periods of time in both Greek history and the history of Rome during which women were freer to exercise power in roles usually reserved by men for themselves, as in Hellenistic Greece and early imperial Rome, they were still under legal disabilities, and their sexuality, directed by their male-dominated societies toward their reproductive roles, was seen as something that needed to be regulated and controlled. One of the ways of doing so was through models held up to women as exemplary of the way they should behave, in literature, through inscriptions, and especially through religious models. As Cantarella also notes, "It is the cults of the ancient female divinities that reveal the role of women most clearly. Often depicted in the act of nursing, the goddess was worshipped as representative and symbol of the woman faithful to her domestic duties."[65]

In which roles, therefore, could women—either real women or idealized women—be seen as saviors in Greco-Roman antiquity? To return to the first model of the savior, the one by whose power an individual, people, or city is saved, it is remarkable that the epithets for "savior" are rarely used for female deities (the Roman Juno and the Greco-Egyptian Isis are notable exceptions), while in the evidence from literature, papyri, and inscriptions—such as public dedications and inscriptions on tombs—there are no instances of the term having been applied to actual women, even women known to have exhibited heroic conduct in saving their cities. Plutarch cites an example of female heroism from the first century B.C.E.—Aretaphila of Cyrene, who successfully contrived to rid Cyrene of its tyrant and his family. For this deed, which involved her survival of torture, the citizens regarded her as a hero and even invited her to take part in their government because of her aristocratic standing as well as her heroic behavior. Aretaphila declined, returning home to the women's quarters, where she remained with her family.[66]

Among the women memorialized as "benefactress" (*euergetes*) in papyri and inscriptions, none of them is described as *soteira* or *sospitatrix* (savior), and all of them are described in terms of traditional female virtue.[67] In an inscription from Asia Minor in the second century C.E., Flavia Publicia Nicomachis, "a benefactor, and benefactor through her ancestors" of her city, is regarded as "founder of our city, president for life," but "in recognition of her complete virtue."[68] Aurelia Leite, "gymnasiarch" of Paros, who repaired the dilapidated city gymnasium at her own expense, is lauded in terms reminiscent of the *'eshet hayil* (woman of worth) praised in Proverbs 31: "She loved wisdom, her husband, her

children, her native city."[69] There are two examples,
both from Asia Minor, both from the third century C.E.,
of a *heroon* being erected by or for a woman (Aurelia
Tryphaena of Smyrna for herself and heirs; Aurelios Zosi-
mos for his wife, Aurelia Syncletica), but it is probable
that *heroon* is used here simply as a term for "tomb,"
perhaps with some sacrifices connected with it, or perhaps to emphasize its inviolability and the divine penalty
attendant on anyone who tries to bury a member of another family in the ancestral tomb.[70] A possible indication
of a heroization of a dead woman is cited by Theodora
Hadzisteliou Price in the context of stelae (tombstones)
that appear to represent the familiar "nursing goddess"
(*kourotrophos*), but that may actually represent the woman
buried there *as* the *kourotrophos* or one of her manifestations. Of eight such stelae that appear in the fourth
and fifth centuries B.C.E., one from Icaria portrays a
woman named Apollonia, who holds a baby girl, while
four other children stand around. The "unusual width"
of the stele, suggests Price, may be due to "a votive
character,... hinting to a kind of heroization of the dead
Apollonia."[71]

Another saving role regarded as particularly appropriate for women is one that appears prominently in Greek
myth. According to Lefkowitz, "Of all the roles played
by women in Greek myth certainly the most active, and
therefore the most deserving of the praise ordinarily ac-
corded to men, is self-sacrifice."[72] The model of heroic
self-sacrifice in Greek mythology is Iphigenia, the inno-
cent virgin who allows herself to be killed so that the
Greeks may be successful against the Trojans. As Euripides represents her in *Iphigenia at Aulis,* she is a willing
victim, conscious of her role in the salvation history of
Greece:

> All Greece turns
> Her eyes to me, to me only, great Greece
> In her might—for through me is the sailing

Of the fleet, through me the sack and overthrow
Of Troy. Because of me, never more will
Barbarians wrong and ravish Greek women,
Drag them from happiness and their homes
In Hellas. The penalty (*olethron*) will be paid
Fully for the shame and seizure of Helen.

And all
These things, all of them, my death will achieve
And accomplish. I, savior (*eleutherosa*) of Greece,
Will win honor and my name shall be blessed.
              (*Iphigenia in Aulis* 1378–84)[73]

Iphigenia is a constellation of the qualities of redeemer and savior: Her death is redemptive; it vicariously pays the penalty for Helen's "shame" (a sexual sin). In a way similar to the cancellation of Eve's fault by Mary's virgin obedience, as seen in the church fathers, Iphigenia's virgin obedience pays the price for the destructive sexuality of the unfaithful Helen. Iphigenia pleads to be the "savior" of Hellas (1420); she also will be, through her death, "Hellas' 'benefactress'" (*euergetis;* 1446). Here, then, is the quintessential female savior as the Greeks envisioned her: the self-sacrificing martyr.

Within the Roman world, mythic and legendary models of female heroism also emphasized sacrifice. Lucretia, the model of the chaste wife, kills herself because of her dishonor and thus sets in motion the chain of events that liberates the Roman Republic from the tyrannical Tarquins (Livy 1.58–60). As Eva Cantarella points out, even the funerary inscriptions of Roman women point out what behavior would win praise from men: primarily keeping the house (*domum servit; domiseda*) and remaining faithful (*pudica; casta; univira*).[74] Many of the inscriptions of upper-class Roman woman reflect their sacrifices during the periods of civil war, especially during the collapse of the Second Triumvirate, in order to preserve the lives of their husbands. The famous *Laudatio Turiae,* or "Praise

of Turia," from the first century B.C.E., eulogizes Turia's
ability to save her husband's life, even while suffering
humiliation and physical abuse from the political leader
Lepidus.[75]

From all of these examples, it would appear that
women are redeemers or saviors not because they exercise power in the way the males of their respective
societies were able to do it—as rulers, warriors, heroes,
and charismatic wonder-workers—but in the way that
contributed nevertheless to the experience of salvation
as the preservation or restoration of life, the giving of
life being a function unique to women as mothers. As
Lefkowitz notes of the models of women in Greek myth,
"At least by stressing the importance of the family and
of women's role within it as nurturers and continuers
of the race, the Greeks attributed to women a vital
function."[76] Women contribute to the sustaining of life,
both through the preservation of their families (and,
by extension, their people) physically, using primarily
the techniques of craft and subterfuge, the only avenues
of power available to them; and through their "keeping" their households by their wise advice or counsel.
Some examples of what men of three eras and three different locales thought praiseworthy in women show a
striking similarity. Semonides, in his infamous satire on
women,[77] nevertheless praises the woman who is "made
from" (i.e., modeled after) the bee: Her activities preserve
her household and family and make them prosper. Semonides's praise recalls that of the "woman of worth" in
Proverbs 31, among the sayings taught to Lemuel by his
mother:

> She is clothed in dignity and in power. . . .
> Her sons with one accord call her happy;
> her husband too, and he sings her praises:
> "Many a woman shows how capable she is;
> but you excel them all."
>   (Prov. 31:25, 28–29, NEB)

An inscription from second-century C.E. Pergamum is strikingly similar: The physician Glycon praises his deceased wife, Panthia, also a physician, for her "beauty, wisdom and chastity" and for her role in "guiding straight the rudder of life" and in "raising high our common fame in healing."[78] We may therefore discern two primary models of female savior figures emerging here: one who saves in and through her various aspects of being a woman and thus may save men as well as women; and one who saves through her sustaining and preserving wisdom. The first may be represented by the universal saving goddess whose worship was at its height in the early centuries of Christianity—Isis, described by her worshipers in terms that can be encapsulated in one dedicatory phrase from Capua, *"tu tibi quae una es omnia* (to you who are all in one)."[79] The second is represented by the figure of Wisdom (*Hokhmah; Sophia*), to whose image certain attributes of Isis became attached in Hellenistic Judaism, and whose attributes are in turn attached to the Christian "mother of salvation," Mary.[80] As Cantarella notes, the religions of Isis and of Christianity were most transformative of women's lives and images in the Greco-Roman world, and at approximately the same time.[81] We might therefore expect to find positive images of women, however male-generated, and perhaps even some traces and outlines of women's responses to those images. Let us turn first to the description of the universal savior as exemplified in a female savior, Isis, in order to examine ways in which a female savior might save both men and women, ways that may prove different from those by which a male savior saves.

Notes

1. Shaye Cohen, *From the Maccabees to the Mishnah*, Library of Early Christianity (Philadelphia: Westminster Press, 1987), 96–97.

2. Joan W. Scott, "Gender: A Useful Category of Historical Analysis," *American Historical Review* 9/15 (1984): 1073.

3. Luther H. Martin, *Hellenistic Religions* (New York: Oxford University Press, 1988), 24.

4. John F. A. Sawyer, *Semantics in Biblical Research*, Studies in Biblical Theology, 2d series, 24 (Naperville, Ill.: Alec R. Allenson, 1972), 112.

5. See Stanislaus Lyonnet, "The Terminology of Redemption," in *Sin, Redemption, and Sacrifice*, ed. S. Lyonnet and L. Sabourin, Analecta biblica, 48 (Rome: Biblical Institute Press, 1970), 59–184.

6. It is interesting to observe that Sawyer does not include either of these terms or their contexts in his study of Hebrew terms for salvation. Apparently, he believes that redemption is at least semantically different from salvation.

7. R. C. Denton, "Redeem, Redeemer, Redemption," *IDB* 4:21–22.

8. The masculine terminology and pronouns are deliberately used here, as they typically denote males only.

9. Denton, "Redeem," *IDB* 4:21–22.

10. See Lev. 25:25, 47–49; Ruth 4:4–6; and Jer. 32:6–12 for the responsibility of the next of kin; Isa. 43:1; 44:22–23; 52:9 for the metaphorical application of this term to YHWH.

11. Cohen, *Maccabees*, 93.

12. Nevertheless, this concept and word are used very sparingly in the New Testament, even in the epistles, where they

are mainly found. This absence suggests that the New Testament writers are working within the paradigm of salvation rather than that of redemption. See Lyonnet, "Terminology of Redemption," 88.

13. For a complete exegesis of the story of the Levite's concubine in Judges 19, see Phyllis Trible, *Texts of Terror* (Philadelphia: Fortress Press, 1985), 64–91.

14. Rita M. Gross, "Steps Toward Feminine Imagery of Deity in Jewish Theology," in *On Being a Jewish Feminist*, ed. Susannah Heschel (New York: Schocken Books, 1983), 236; see Judith Plaskow, "The Right Question *Is* Theological," in Heschel, ed., *On Being a Jewish Feminist*, 223–33.

15. Plaskow, "The Right Question," 225.

16. See Sawyer, *Semantics*, 102–11.

17. Ibid., 109–10.

18. James Barr, "An Aspect of Salvation in the Old Testament," in *Man and His Salvation: Studies in Honor of S. G. F. Brandon*, ed. Eric J. Sharpe and John R. Hinnells (Manchester: Manchester University Press, 1973), 39–52.

19. Ibid., 47–51.

20. Ibid., 45.

21. G. Fohrer and W. Foerster, "Sozo," *TDNT* 7:1004.

22. Martin, *Hellenistic Religions*, 24.

23. Fohrer and Foerster, "Sozo," *TDNT* 7:1004.

24. Lyonnet, "Terminology of Redemption," 68.

25. Barr, "Aspect," 48.

26. George W. Nickelsburg, *Jewish Literature Between the Bible and the Mishnah* (Philadelphia: Fortress Press, 1981), 106–7.

27. Claudia V. Camp, *Wisdom and the Feminine in the Book of Proverbs*, Bible and Literature Series, 11 (Sheffield: JSOT/ Almond Press, 1985), 124.

28. Ibid., 228; see Burton Mack, *Logos und Sophia: Untersuchungen zur Weisheitstheologie im hellenistischen Judentum*, Studien zur Umwelt des Neuen Testaments, 10 (Göttingen: Vandenhoeck & Ruprecht, 1973), 29–32.

29. Mack, *Logos und Sophia*, 75–76, 285.

30. Toni Craven, *Artistry and Faith in the Book of Judith*, SBLDS, 70 (Chico, Calif.: Scholars Press, 1983), 4.

31. Carey A. Moore, *Judith: A New Translation with Introduction, Notes, and Commentary*, Anchor Bible (Garden City, N.Y.: Doubleday, 1985), 64.

32. Martin, *Hellenistic Religions*, 90.

33. Cited by Moore, *Judith*, 64.

34. William Scott Green, "Messiah in Judaism," in *Judaisms and Their Messiahs at the Turn of the Christian Era*, ed. Jacob Neusner, William Scott Green, and Ernest Frerichs (Cambridge and New York: Cambridge University Press, 1987), 2–3.

35. Ibid., 5.

36. Hyam Maccoby, *The Mythmaker: Paul and the Invention of Christianity* (New York: Harper & Row, 1986), 184.

37. Charles H. Talbert, "The Myth of a Descending-ascending Redeemer in Mediterranean Antiquity," *NTS* 22 (1976): 420.

38. Ibid., 421.

39. Jacob Neusner, *The Incarnation of God: The Character of Divinity in Formative Judaism* (Philadelphia: Fortress Press, 1988), 188.

40. Richard D. Hecht, "Philo and Messiah," in Neusner, Green, and Frerichs, eds., *Judaisms*, 149.

41. David Grene and Richmond Lattimore, eds., *Greek Tragedies*, vol. 1, trans. Elizabeth Wyckoff (Chicago: University of Chicago Press, 1966), 187.

42. Fohrer and Foerster, "Sozo," *TDNT* 7:973–80.

43. Isis-aretalogy from Kyme-Memphis, *Inscriptiones graecae, supplementum* (1939), 98–99 (cited by A. J. Festugière, "À propos des arètalogies d'Isis," *HTR* 42/2 [1949]: 223).

44. A. A. Long, ed., *Problems in Stoicism* (London: University of London/Athlone Press, 1971), 177–95.

45. Martin, *Hellenistic Religions*, 35.

46. C. J. Bleeker, "Isis as Saviour Goddess," in *The Saviour God: Comparative Studies in the Concept of Salvation: Presented by Edwin Oliver James*, ed. S. G. F. Brandon (Manchester: Manchester University Press, 1963), 2.

47. Fohrer and Foerster, "Sozo," *TDNT* 7:1004.

48. Ibid., 7:1005.

49. Ibid., 7:1005–9.

50. See my "Power and the Man of Power in Hellenistic Popular Belief," *Helios*, n.s., 13/1 (1986): 75–86; and Peter Brown, *The Making of Late Antiquity* (Cambridge, Mass.: Harvard University Press, 1978), 12, for discussions of the connection of power with divinity and of the concept of embodied power.

51. See Ludwig Bieler, *THEIOS ANER* (1935–36; reprint, Darmstadt: Wissenschaftliche Buchgesellschaft, 1967), for the primary statement of this "type" as applied to Jesus in the New Testament; see my *The "Divine Man": His Origin and Function in Hellenistic Popular Religion,* American University Studies, 8:17 (Bern and New York: Peter Lang, 1986), especially 1–58, for an outline of research on this figure.

52. Fohrer and Foerster, "Sozo," *TDNT* 7:1007.

53. Moses Hadas and Morton Smith, *Heroes and Gods: Spiritual Biographies in Antiquity,* Religious Perspectives, 13 (New York: Harper & Row, 1965), 10.

54. Ibid., 11.

55. *Etymologicum Magnum,* s.v. "Dexion," in David G. Rice and John E. Stambaugh, *Sources for the Study of Greek Religion,* Sources for Biblical Study, 14 (Missoula, Mont.: Scholars Press, 1979), 65–66.

56. Martin P. Nilsson, *Greek Popular Religion* (New York: Columbia University Press, 1940), 20.

57. Plutarch, *Life of Cleomenes* (cited by Hadas and Smith, *Heroes and Gods,* 80).

58. See H. Haerens, "Soter et soteria," *Studia hellenistica* 5 (1948): 57–58.

59. Rice and Stambaugh, *Sources,* 65.

60. Mary R. Lefkowitz, *Women in Greek Myth* (Baltimore: Johns Hopkins University Press, 1986), 30.

61. Ibid.

62. Rosemary R. Ruether, *Mary, the Feminine Face of the Church* (Philadelphia: Westminster Press, 1977), 17.

63. Eva Cantarella, *Pandora's Daughters: The Role and Status of Women in Greek and Roman Antiquity,* trans. Maureen B. Fant (Baltimore: Johns Hopkins University Press, 1987), 39.

64. Ibid., 101.

65. Ibid., 109.

66. Plutarch, *Moral Essays* 257 D–E (cited by and trans. Lefkowitz, *Women in Greek Myth,* 88).

67. Ibid.

68. Mary R. Lefkowitz and Maureen B. Fant, *Women's Life in Greece and Rome: A Source Book in Translation* (Baltimore: Johns Hopkins University Press, 1982), no. 162.

69. Lefkowitz and Fant, *Women's Life,* no. 164.

70. Examples taken from Ross S. Kraemer, ed., *Maenads, Martyrs, Matrons, and Monastics: A Sourcebook on Women's Religions in the Greco-Roman World* (Philadelphia: Fortress Press, 1988), nos. 55 and 57.

71. Theodora Hadzisteliou Price, *Kourotrophos: Cults and Representations of Greek Nursing Deities* (Leiden: E. J. Brill, 1978), 46.

72. Lefkowitz, *Women in Greek Myth*, 95.

73. David Grene and Richmond Lattimore, eds., *The Complete Greek Tragedies*, vol. 4: *Euripides*, trans. Charles R. Walker (Chicago: University of Chicago Press, 1958), 290.

74. Cantarella, *Pandora's Daughters*, 130–33.

75. Lefkowitz and Fant, *Women's Life*, no. 207.

76. Lefkowitz, *Women in Greek Myth*, 46, 129.

77. Fragment 7W, Lefkowitz and Fant, *Women's Life*, no. 30.

78. Lefkowitz and Fant, *Women's Life*, no. 125.

79. Ladislaus Vidman, *Sylloge inscriptionum religionis Isiacae et Sarapicae* (Berlin: Walter de Gruyter, 1969), no. 502.

80. Ruether, *Mary*, 18, 27.

81. Cantarella, *Pandora's Daughters*, 158.

2

Patterns of Power:
The Universal Savior

> Holy and eternal savior of the human race, ever
> beneficent in cherishing mortals, you indeed bestow
> the sweet affection of a mother upon the tribulations
> of the unfortunate.
> —Apuleius, *Metamorphoses* 11.25

The Promise of Universal Salvation

As Mircea Eliade has expressed it, the great religions that developed in the Mediterranean world in the
three centuries preceding the common era addressed a
widely perceived need with a nearly universal answer:
"the promise of salvation."[1] Enacting this promise took

two main forms: salvation *out* of this world through deliverance or rescue from the hostile powers like those of Fate, Fortune, and Limit; and salvation as transformation of status *within* this world. James M. Fennelly attributes the success of Christianity to its ability to address the need for freedom from the constraints of "Roman economic determinism" and the "rigid social structure" and its ability to restore a sense of "class mobility and group acceptance," together with a sense of identity in the group as well as in the universe.[2] Such a universal religion of salvation needed to dissolve the old limits of regions, classes, and other structures, some of which had already perished, and to create new associations.

Yet there were religions of salvation that had attempted to do just those things before the triumph of Christianity. These were primarily the mystery religions, which promised eternal blessedness to the faithful through identification with a deity. At the end of the Hellenistic period, and by the beginning of the first century, the title "savior" (*soter*) was being used for the deities of these religions, who were increasingly described in a "syncretized and universal" fashion.[3] The universality and syncretistic nature of the deity was often accompanied by a "deepening or extending of pre-existing piety through a new intimacy with the divine in both familiar and novel shapes."[4] This "intimacy with the divine" took the shape of identification with the deity of the mystery religion, either as participant in his or her divinity (through symbolic action, sacred meal, or by possession, as in the Dionysiac mysteries), or as the adopted "child" of the deity. The saving deity, as previously noted, was therefore connected with human life in an intimate way: as mediator between the divine and human realms, as combining human and divine characteristics, and as transforming the status of the worshiper into that of "salvation" (that is, offering the worshiper safety, health, and security).[5]

Such an intimate connection between the divine and human realm, moreover, might also be expected to involve questions of personal identity and orientation. It has been suggested that one of the reasons for the increase in adherence to salvation religions, including the mysteries, in the Hellenistic and Greco-Roman periods was the continuing decay and collapse of old structures of identification and orientation, from the top to the bottom.[6] Like all new or revivalist religious movements, salvation religions are indicators of "social conflict and the search for social integration,... psychic revolt and the quest for meaning."[7] While the role of social conflict in the development of Christianity has been fairly exhaustively explored, the exploration has tended to emphasize Christianity's *uniqueness* rather than characteristics it shares with other religious movements of the period.

Questions of identity and integration inevitably involve questions of gender, among other factors like class and race. It is certainly true that, as Ross Kraemer has observed, "Goddesses are not per se the objects of women's devotion, nor do they by definition reflect women's perceptions of themselves and the universe in which they live."[8] It is also the case that, particularly for earlier periods of history, texts generated by women are almost entirely lacking; further, the few texts that contain female metaphors and images for divinity either cannot be conclusively proven to have been written by women or were almost certainly written by men to valorize certain male-generated images of women. Indeed, descriptions of women's religious activities during these time periods have nearly all been authored by men, often in the interest of polemics against such activities. Nor can we be sure that there is always a direct "correlation between the gender of the deity and the gender of the deity's officiants."[9] Nevertheless, as Caroline Walker Bynum has suggested, women and men do react differently to gendered religious symbols: "Women's symbols and myths tend to build from social and biological experiences; men's symbols and myths tend to invert them."[10] Thus, if a goddess is presented primarily in the roles of wife, sister, and mother, as are both Isis and Sophia (Wisdom), such roles, although limited by the texts in which they are presented, might be expected to be viewed by women as continuous in some way with their own social and biological roles and experiences.

Are such distinctions preserved or obscured in religions that promise universal salvation? Let us take as examples two such religions that Eva Cantarella posits had a role in changing the image of women particularly: the Isis religion and Christianity.[11] The Egyptian goddess Isis in her Greco-Roman personification was the focus of a religion that had both an elite and a popular manifestation, the latter making it one of the most widespread religions of the early centuries of the common era. It became one of Christianity's "unfortunate rivals," especially in Egypt, where its popular nature, its connection with the resurrection of Osiris, and its persistent tendency toward monotheism, according to Jean Leclant, "prepared for Christianity."[12] R. E. Witt, in fact, claims that Isis "made the same universal appeal" to varying genders and classes as did Paul's version of Christianity.[13] While such a statement may be a somewhat imaginative interpretation of the facts, it nevertheless points to an important point of comparison between the two religions: the attempt of the preaching and propaganda of both to present them as universal. Paul, in fact, as noted above, was instrumental in translating Christianity from its origins as an eschatological, rural, Palestinian movement to a Greco-Roman religion of universal salvation; similarly, the propaganda of the Isis aretalogies proclaimed her "ruler of every land" and "holy and eternal savior of the human race."[14]

While we will examine in more detail the portrayal of the savior and of salvation in these two religions, especially as related to gender, we must first outline what is meant by their appeal to universality. The religion of Isis was universal in that participation in it was not restricted to those who—like Lucius, the hero of Apuleius of Madaura's "Isiac" novel—could afford the "rare event" of initiation into the complete mysteries; nor were these initiations the center of Isis worship.[15] Unlike the mysteries of Demeter and Kore, where participants had at minimum to speak and understand Greek, the religion of Isis was potentially open to all nationalities, and indeed was found throughout the empire in the early centuries of the common era. Both men and women participated in the religious ritual, both as officiants[16] and as worshipers. Indeed, as Sharon Kelly Heyob notes, "A very strong laity was a characteristic of the Isiac cult."[17] Because the religion originated in Egypt, it might be expected that its clergy was primarily Egyptian, and the evidence of inscriptions and the wall paintings of Isiac ritual found at Herculaneum suggests that both native Egyptian and non-Egyptian worshipers and officiants took part in the ceremonies of the religion.[18] Social status, too, seemed to have meant little in terms of admission to the Isis religion. In Roman Egypt, it preserved its popular character, as indicated by the numbers of terra-cotta dedications from people, especially from women, of the Egyptian countryside.[19] When the religion came to Rome, it, like other foreign religions, tended to locate itself among tradespeople and the lower classes. This adherence of the non-elite to the Isis religion was regarded as subversive by the Roman senatorial class, which persecuted and banned worship of Isis in Rome itself a number of times during the Republic and the early empire.[20] What occasioned the most spectacular persecution of the Isis religion during the reign of Tiberius in 19 C.E., however, provides an echo of the violent suppression of the Bacchic worship over two hundred years earlier (246 B.C.E.): the possible sexual misbehavior of an upper-class Roman matron, Paulina (Josephus, *Jewish Antiquities* 18.65–80), which resulted in the crucifixion of the Isis priests and the "drowning" of Isis's statue in the Tiber. This took place despite the reputation of the deity for marital fidelity and chastity, a reputation lauded even by the church fathers,[21] and despite the fact that enforced periods of sexual abstinence required by the religion were known (and lamented) by the elegiac poets of the time (see Tibullus, 1.3.29–32; Propertius, 2.33.1–4).

A similar situation existed with respect to Christianity. In the earliest Christian community of which we have traces in the Gospels, the community that produced the collection of Jesus' sayings known as Q,[22] a radical social and sexual egalitarianism was practiced, along with a high regard for Wisdom as an aspect of the divine that was especially revealed by her envoy, Jesus.[23] Jesus' preaching about the community of the end, according to Paula Fredriksen, emphasized a universal judgment, but also offered universal redemption of "former sinners, scattered Israel, and ultimately even the no longer idolatrous gentiles."[24] In Paul's epistles, traces of this former radical egalitarianism remain, tempered however by the exigencies of persons practicing a nonlegal religion whose life-style might appear suspicious and subversive in the eyes of the Roman authorities. In Galatians, Paul sets aside the Law, which for him was the chief dividing line between Jew and Gentile, and he announces the erasure of ethnic, gender, and status boundaries "in Christ," using the language of participation: "For as many of you who have been baptized into Christ have put on Christ; for one is not Jew and one Greek; one is not slave and one free; one is not male and one female; but all of you are one in Christ Jesus" (Gal. 3:27–28). In Romans, Paul uses the theme of universal salvation to demonstrate the universal condemnation of humanity under a righteous God, its consequent need to be redeemed, and its redemption being achieved through the death of Christ: "For all have sinned and come short of the glory of God, being freely made righteous by his grace through the redemption [*apolytrosis*] that is in Christ Jesus" (Rom. 3:23–24). His point here, however, is that there is no differentiation (*diastole*) between Jews and Greeks. He does not include other differences—such as those between slave and free, male and female, although he uses terminology of slavery and marriage as metaphors—because his main emphasis is on finding whatever role there remains for the Law with the inclusion of the Gentiles in God's universal plan of salvation: "For there is no distinction [*diastole*] between Jew and Greek, for he is master [*kyrios*] of all, generous to all who call upon him" (Rom. 10:12). God is here seen in the figure of the generous Roman patron or benefactor.

In the letter to the church at Corinth, Paul also abandons a significant portion of his erasure of boundaries. While using the terminology of the body and its unity to quell the factions (*schismata*) that had sprung up in the congregation, presumably over ranking within categories of Spirit possession and therefore authority, he does not abandon one distinction that he believes should remain: that of male and female in the worship service. Needing language for communal unity, he reiterates the language of Galatians 3:27–28 in 1 Corinthians 12:12–13: "For just as the body is one and has many limbs, but all the limbs of the body, though many, are one body, it is the same way with Christ. For in one Spirit we all were baptized into one body, whether Jew or Greek, whether slave or free, and we were all given to drink one Spirit." The glaring lack of the "male or female" distinction is explained by a passage in the previous chapter (11:2–16) in which Paul makes use of a perceived "natural" hierarchy of order and control, in which women keep their heads covered. Those who are uncovered and therefore "out of control," perhaps in the ecstasy of prophetic speech, bring shame upon their "heads," their husbands. It was a natural step, then, for the post-Pauline editor of this text to add to the instructions on orderly worship in 1 Corinthians 14:26–33 the injunction for women to keep silent and be subordinate to their husbands (14:34–36).

Paul's anxiety over the decorum of the congregation in Corinth, especially of its female members, is not unusual, given the attitude of the Roman authorities. Paul, after all, was a leader of a new, possibly suspect religious movement that attracted women of affluence and presumably influence, among other persons of the artisan and lower classes. The behavior of women in the worship of Isis also came in for a certain amount of attention from Apuleius: He emphasizes the fact that those women who took part in the public rites had a "light covering" upon their heads (*Metamorphoses* 11.10), as befitting modest Roman matrons. Thus both authors have an apologetic motive in referring to proper dress and behavior for the female believers in their respective religions; their motive was to avoid bringing upon them the ire of the Roman authorities by any suspicion of sexual impropriety, located in "uncontrolled" female behavior. Ironically, this protectiveness resulted, at least in the case of later Christian women, in their being suppressed by the very religion that first appeared to promise them some freedom from their customary sociobiological roles. The ideal of virginity in Christianity, which appeared to exalt women (because they "became men") and to free them from the "curse of Eve" (painful childbirth as the result of sexual intercourse), was an impossible ideal for most women to achieve. Indeed, the writings of Paul's followers in the second century reflect the attempt to confine women once more to flesh and matter: The writer of 1 Timothy sees women as "saved" by childbirth, but only if they also "behave" themselves decorously and modestly (1 Tim. 2:8–15). Women are not to be included in the office of teaching or other offices that give them authority over men; nor are they apparently even to pray publicly. The only stated "order" for women, that of widows, is subject to regulation and control to prevent criticism from the outside world (5:3–16). In short, the rising orthodox church order of the second century reflects the situation in the larger society, in which the economic crises and falling birth rate in the Roman upper classes led to an increasing resubordination of women and the return, according to Cantarella, to the "negative image" of woman as "flesh and matter" and fallen flesh at that.[25]

Hence, in the development of Pauline theology, as it took place within the Greco-Roman social world, the equality of women as promised "in Christ" was early eroded by the formation of two models for women. In the first, the unmarried woman (virgin or widow) was exalted, resulting in the denigration of "dangerous" female sexuality. This model, as Lefkowitz points out, actually "offered to virgins a new subservience rather than increased independence."[26] In the second, the woman as wife and mother was clearly subordinate, in creation as well as salvation, to the man, her "head" as husband and father. Even if she dresses and acts modestly, remains chaste, faithful, and "holy," and is "saved" by the further step of bearing children, her subordination in the community of Christ is a reminder that Eve, the first transgressor, was also a wife (Adam's) and was punished for her "deception" by being ruled by him and having pain as a mother.

The Savior Goddess?

If in early Christian thinking women are seen as *saved* by becoming mothers, in the worship of Isis, the goddess is salvific precisely *because* she is a mother, and as such she both embodies and exalts women as mothers as well as wives. Isis's very origins in Egypt, like her manifestations in the Hellenistic and Greco-Roman periods, reflect these two major roles: that of wife and that of mother. In both of these, Isis functions as the giver and sustainer of life. In her first appearance in Egyptian mythology, Isis was the incarnation of the pharaoh's "throne" ('*aset*). As the throne symbolically "created" or "gave birth to" the pharaoh, so Isis, the incarnate throne, was the mother of the pharaoh.[27] But the throne is also the *lap* and hence the *womb* of the divine mother's body. Isis is the nursing mother who through her breasts imparts the "milk of salvation" to the king, when he is born, when he is enthroned, and when he dies, in order to give him new life in the next world.[28] The role of Isis as nursing mother enabled her to be combined with, and identified as, other maternal deities in Egypt, like Hathor, who loaned her cow's horns to Isis's own iconography even as she "shared" temples and attributes with the goddess.

But Isis was seen as the conqueror of death and the divine giver of life because of her devotion to, and resurrection of, her husband-brother Osiris, and because of her androgynous conception of her son Horus and her protection of him from Seth's assaults on his life. According to the myth of Isis and Osiris, the goddess, lamenting over the death and dismemberment of her husband by his brother, Seth (or Typhon), faithfully gathered all of the pieces of his dead body (except for the phallus). She mummified and then magically revived the body, whereupon she made a phallus out of the magical materials of saliva and mud, and lit upon it in the shape of a bird, in order to conceive Horus, whom she protected from Seth by hiding him in the rushes of the Nile.[29] Isis was therefore connected with giving life, both to Osiris and to Horus, and eventually to all of the dead who were her devotees. She thus became their common "mother," the genetrix of life after death.

When the worship of Isis spread throughout the Mediterranean, beginning as early as the eighth century before the common era, the image of Isis nursing her infant son became conflated in the minds of the Greeks, as it had been with the Egyptians, with that of other nursing deities.[30] The image of the nursing infant Horus, originally the symbol of the pharaoh receiving immortality from his divine mother, became that of the "infant" soul about to be regenerated through its connection with the milk from the breast of the divine mother. As Theodora H. Price has observed, this divine milk is the means by which not only kings and heroes, but also initiates in the mystery religions, receive eternal life: "The sacramental act of nursing, symbolic of divine adoption, protection, or initiation as a means of divinity, is found in the Eleusinian, Orphic, and later Sabazian mysteries."[31] Indeed, the attributes of Isis became combined with those of Demeter, that other divine regenerating mother, as demonstrated by Plutarch's conflation of the myths of nursing in his *On Isis and Osiris* (351; see Herodotus, *Histories* 2.59, 123).

Yet we might well ask whether this model, generated from the time of the Pyramid Texts and transformed during the Greek takeover of Egypt in the fourth century B.C.E., is capable of admitting or describing genuine female experiences. Indeed, it would at first appear as though much of the propaganda of Isis worship, carried as it was throughout the Hellenistic and Greco-Roman worlds by male priests, proselytizers, and merchants, has less to do with the experiences and needs of actual women than it does with their idealization as spouses and mothers. In the theology of Isis, as in the theology of Wisdom, with whom she shares several attributes, there are two levels: One is the royal theology, with Isis as the protectress of rulers and sponsor of laws and cities; the other is the more common theology, in which Isis is protectress of men in her role as mother, lover, sister, and spouse, and of women as woman in all of her passages through life and her many transformations. As R. E. Witt notes:

In her the believer could discern the warm affection of the bereaved wife, the tenderness of the mother suckling her baby, ... the concern of the midwife for the safe delivery in childbirth, the sexual passion symbolized by the . . . erect phallus and by the legend that she had played the harlot for ten years at Tyre.[32]

The image of a real mother or nurse with her child is evident even in the origins of the Isis figure, who is one of the very few deities of Egypt to remain gynomorphic (woman in form) rather than theriomorphic (animal in form) throughout her long history. It would appear as though the official or royal iconography of Isis has in fact been derived from popular representations, arising in the popular imagination, rather than the reverse.[33] Françoise Dunand notes of popular figurines related to the Isis religion in Roman Egypt that it is difficult to determine whether they are representations of the deity herself or representations of Egyptian mothers that were used as a form of thanks for successful childbirth and child-rearing:

> Here are familiar poses, imprinted with those of the women of Egypt. . . . The same transposition to the divine realm of the gestures of daily life appears in a bronze from the Berlin Museum . . . dating from the Middle Kingdom [Egyptian Museum, Berlin, Inv. no. 14078, ca. 1900 B.C.E.], in which one sees Isis, sitting on the ground, one knee bent, nursing her son in the manner of an Egyptian peasant woman.[34]

But woman as mother was not the only incarnation of Isis, even if it was her most salient one. In the longest and probably the most famous of her aretalogies (praise-litanies), that of Kyme-Memphis, Isis's self-revelation characterizes her in terms that are descriptive both of her royal functions (as *kyria*, mistress; *tyrannos* and *despoina*, ruler) and of her relational functions (as wife, daughter, sister, and deity of women). Although she is the one who orders the universe through discovering the paths of the stars and planets, is the inventress of writing and seafaring, and is the lawgiver (*nomothetes; thesmophoros*) and

embodiment of justice (*dikaiosyne*), she is also characterized as a woman. She is "eldest daughter of Kronos (Re),"
the "wife and sister" of Osiris, and the mother of Horus. She identifies herself as "the one who is called deity
(*theos*, the masculine form) by women." She is the one who
"brought together" woman and man; the one who causes
women to give birth in the tenth month; and the one who
"laid it down for parents to be loved by their children"
and who punishes children who do not have affection
for their parents. Finally, she is the one who "compelled
women to be loved by men."[35]

In the Isis aretalogy in the Oxyrhynchus papyrus (*P.
Oxy.* 11.1380), dating from the second century C.E., Isis
is invoked in syncretistic fashion by various titles that
point to her lawgiving, her sponsorship of rulers, and her
"many shapes" and "many names." She is invoked, then,
in truly universal fashion. Yet here too she is the one who
wills "that women in health come to anchor with men";
the one who is worshiped by unmarried women at Hera-
cleopolis; and most importantly, the one who "didst make
the power of women equal to that of men."[36] Apuleius of
Madaura, also writing in the second century, describes
Isis worship in the eleventh book of his novel, the *Metamorphoses*. There he makes it abundantly clear that Isis,
through her conquest of Fortune, is the sole universal
savior of the human race in the midst of its folly and its
suffering. Lucius, the protagonist of the novel, experi-
ments with magic and witchcraft and creates his suffering
by literally turning himself into an ass. Isis manifests herself to him as his savior: "I am here, having taken pity on
your misfortunes; I am here, with favor and with solace"
(*Metamorphoses* 11.15). As a result of this epiphany and its
aftermath, his transformation back into a human being
and his assurance of eternal life, Lucius realizes that Isis
is the "savioress" (*sospitatrix*) of all of humanity, who saves
precisely in her role as mother (*mater*): "Holy and eternal
savioress of the human race, ever beneficent in cherish-
ing mortals, you indeed bestow the sweet affection of a

mother upon the tribulations of the unfortunate" (11.25). Thus we may see that, even in texts presumably reflecting the interests of male authors, Isis is praised not only in her cosmic and royal dimensions, but also as sacred to women, as protective of them, and as granting them a power equal to that of men.

In the dedications, inscriptions, and funerary monuments of women throughout the Greco-Roman world, moreover, we have further evidence that women of all levels of society might find in Isis not only their own embodiment and a protectress and participant in every passage of their lives, but also one who is so by virtue of the very aspects males of their society found most limiting of women: marriage and childbirth. In the exercise of female sexuality itself, Isis was a powerful deity, as evidenced by her conflation with Hathor, Egyptian goddess of fertility and "wild" (uncontrolled) sexuality, with the Syrian Goddess (Dea Syria), and with Aphrodite in the Greek world. But, as Heyob notes, Isis was particularly attractive to women in the Greco-Roman world because she was "a model for inspiration in the circumstances of domestic life," and was especially endeared to "that class of society whose concerns revolved around domestic life."[37] The popularity of the image of Isis nursing the infant Horus—as attested by numerous dedicatory figurines, amulets for protection, lamp handles (also for protection?), and magical gems—appears to have originated in the need of the women of Egypt, echoed by their sisters in the rest of the Greco-Roman world. In the words of Paul Perdrizet: "The women of Egypt, . . . by dint of imploring the goddess-mother and her divine infant, ended by setting them up as principal and essential divinities."[38] That Isis protected other aspects of female life is indicated by three titles used of her only by women: Isis *bubastis* (women of childbearing age); Isis *puellaris* (girls before menstruation); and Isis *lochia* (women in child-bed). Isis-knots—representing the knot tying the girdle of the garment of the Greco-Roman Isis, itself de-

rived from the Egyptian *ankh*, the symbol of life and
the sun—were made of red jasper to relieve menstrual
cramps, attesting to the power of the goddess as healer
and magician.[39]

But, as Heyob notes and as numerous inscriptions and
funerary stelae bear out, "Women in particular seem
to have found great comfort in the *redemptive aspects* of
the religion."[40] Since imitation of the goddess by women
seems to have been an important part of the public cel-
ebrations attendant on worship of Isis, it is not at all
unexpected that portraits of women arrayed with the dis-
tinctive ornaments of Isis (dress gathered in an Isis-knot;
carrying a *sistrum*, a musical instrument used in worship;
often carrying a *sistula*, a pail for sprinkling water; and
wearing a crescent moon in the hair) would appear on
their funerary monuments.[41] This "putting on" of the
goddess, presumably as an indication of participation in
her deity and hence of the assurance of a good life after death, appears not to be limited only to priestesses,
officiants, or initiates in the religion. In one example of
a stele from Roman Egypt, Seratous, a twenty-one-year-
old woman, is not only depicted in the dress of Isis and
in a pose familiar from many iconographic representations of the goddess (offering her breast to a child whose
hand she also holds), but is described in terms of praise
reminiscent of the epithets of Isis herself. Like Isis, she
appears to speak for herself: She reveals her identity as
"brother-loving" (*philadelphos*) and as "justice" (*themis*),
reserving her actual name, Seratous, until the end of
the inscription. Isis was celebrated for her devotion to
her husband-brother, Osiris, for which reason Tran Tam
Tinh believes that Seratous was perhaps married in the
Egyptian fashion to her brother, with whom she is also
buried, together with her (their?) mother.[42] Perhaps Seratous, like Isis, is envisioned here as the giver of life, not
only to her child in this world, but also to her brother in
the next. Her epitaph mentions that she is "his greatest
proclamation (*kerygma*)," a claim that is hard to interpret,

but which suggests that she is responsible in some way for his undying fame. She also is self-described as "justice," a title that was a common one for Isis,[43] probably because from her earliest incarnation in Egypt, she was associated with Ma'at, justice personified, and because she was believed to be present at the "weighing of the heart" after death, the Egyptian version of final judgment.

Another stele is even more provocative because it has no inscription. It dates from Christianized Egypt, where the worship of Isis, especially as a healing goddess, continued well into the sixth century, when it was violently suppressed by Cyril, the bishop of Alexandria. This representation, from 500–700 C.E. (Staatliche Museum Berlin, Inv. no. 14726), shows a seated woman nursing her child, and has been taken to portray not only the woman whom it putatively commemorates, but also the goddess Isis, a *kourotrophos* (Greek nursing deity), and Mary with the infant Jesus.[44] The confusion over who exactly this stele represents is not surprising, considering the tendency of women to see themselves and to be represented as partaking of the goddess, even as she partook of their own lives. As the mother imparts life to the child, so the mother Isis imparted life beyond death to her devotees, who were considered her "children." Tran Tam Tinh makes a final, intriguing comment on this stele, which indicates that the identification of women with divine maternal figures, connected with their salvation from death, continued after the suppression of Isis worship in Egypt: "It is difficult to confirm whether the Virgin and child are represented in this funerary imagery; in effect, if the Isiac Seratous . . . presents herself as Isis, our Christianized women of Egypt could have continued this tradition in a 'Christianized' form."[45] It would certainly not have been surprising if the Christian women of Egypt had found another divine mother with whom to identify; the Christian women of Arabia, to Epiphanius's consternation, did a similar thing in their worship of Mary rather than Jesus (Epiphanius, *Medicine Box* 88).

The "cakes" (*kollybas*) offered by the Collyridians to Mary in this worship are described in a way similar to the cakes offered Isis as the "queen of heaven" by Diodorus Siculus (1.14).

Although these examples can only be taken to be indicative, not conclusive, as is typical of the scarce evidence for women's lives and experiences in the ancient world, they do indicate that some women at least regarded Isis's power over life and death as originating in her being, though divine, a mother very much like themselves, concerned for her human children's welfare. This power also became translated, for women as well as for men, into terms descriptive of power and authority available within their social and political world. As previously indicated, Isis was addressed as "mistress" (*kyria, domina, despoina*), and also with male titles of authority that remain grammatically "unfeminized" in the Kyme-Memphis aretalogy: "ruler" (*tyrannos*) and "master" (*kyrios*). According to Apuleius, her "true" name was "queen" (*regina; Metamorphoses* 11.5). It is by this and similar titles, like *Augusta* (revered lady), that Isis was most frequently addressed by women within the Roman world.[46] We could interpret this form of address in two ways. First, it might be that women were using titles of authority familiar to them from the sociopolitical realm and applying them, as was common also for men, to Isis as a deity of power. Second, it could be that Isis, who "made the power of women equal to that of men," ruled precisely because she, as a mother, had command over life and death. Thus an image continuous with women's own experiences—that of the mother—was understood by them to be one of authority and power, both in this world and the world beyond. Although the image described women in terms of this-worldly power, power that could be enjoyed by ruling queens and influential women, the exercise of such power would have been extraordinary even in their cases, for it was a power that was unattainable by most women.

The difficulty inherent in seeing Isis as a female savior figure is that, in comparison with the Christian savior, she is not incarnate in any particular historical personage; this is true no matter how much she is viewed as incarnate in and embodying women, particularly in the female life cycle. This "difficulty" is of course created only when one views Isis as a savior from a particular Christian perspective. In terms of women's views of their own salvation, it may be that the many incarnations of a saving deity are more capable of being universal than any one incarnation, especially if it is understood in a personal and therefore inevitably gendered way. It is undeniable that this difficulty arises in Christianity, as it does in Judaism, because of the monotheistic nature of these religions. It does not arise in polytheistic or even monistic religions. Nevertheless, there seems to have been a persistent tendency in Judaism and especially in Christianity to pluralize the personae of the deity, even if this pluralization meant a delicate theological balance had to be maintained to prevent a lapse from true monotheism into "idolatry." Ironically, this balancing act led to the denial of certain ways of representing the deity. Such a theological dilemma occurred for Judaism in its understanding of Wisdom as an attribute of the deity, and eventually precluded this undoubtedly female hypostasis from being fully actualized in female humanity. Nonetheless, Wisdom as a saving figure shares many attributes with Isis. Some of these attributes come from, and are incarnated in, the lives of actual women. Hence it is to Wisdom as savior and "firstborn of all creation" that we must now direct our attention.

Notes

1. Mircea Eliade, *A History of Religious Ideas*, vol. 2: *From Gautama Buddha to the Triumph of Christianity* (Chicago: University of Chicago Press, 1982), 277.

2. James M. Fennelly, "The Primitive Christian Values of Salvation and Patterns of Conversion," in *Man and His Salvation: Studies in Honor of S. G. F. Brandon*, ed. Eric J. Sharpe and John R. Hinnells (Manchester: Manchester University Press, 1973), 107–23.

3. H. Haerens, "Soter et soteria," *Studia hellenistica* 5 (1948): 58.

4. Walter Burkert, *Ancient Mystery Cults* (Cambridge, Mass.: Harvard University Press, 1987), 50.

5. C. J. Bleeker, "Isis as Saviour Goddess," in *The Saviour God: Comparative Studies in the Concept of Salvation: Presented by Edwin Oliver James*, ed. S. G. F. Brandon (Manchester: Manchester University Press, 1963), 2.

6. Fennelly, "Primitive Christian Values," 115–23.

7. Henry A. Green, "The Socio-economic Background of Christianity in Egypt," in *The Roots of Egyptian Christianity*, ed. Birger A. Pearson and James E. Goehring, Studies in Antiquity and Christianity (Philadelphia: Fortress Press, 1986), 110.

8. Ross S. Kraemer, ed., *Maenads, Martyrs, Matrons, and Monastics: A Sourcebook on Women's Religions in the Greco-Roman World* (Philadelphia: Fortress Press, 1988), 333.

9. Ibid., 208.

10. Caroline W. Bynum, "Introduction: The Complexity of Symbols," in *Gender and Religion: On the Complexity of Symbols*, ed. Caroline Walker Bynum, Stevan Harrell, and Paula Richman (Boston: Beacon Press, 1986), 13.

11. See Eva Cantarella, *Pandora's Daughters: The Role and Status of Women in Greek and Roman Antiquity*, trans. Maureen B. Fant (Baltimore: Johns Hopkins University Press, 1987), 156–58.

12. Jean Leclant, "Préface" to France Le Corsu, *Isis: Mythe et Mystères* (Paris: Les "Belles Lettres," 1977), ix. All translations into English are mine.

13. R. E. Witt, "The Importance of Isis for the Fathers," *Studia patristica*, 8, *Texte und Untersuchungen zur Geschichte der altchristlichen Literatur* 93 (1966): 137.

14. Kyme-Memphis aretalogy, written by Diodorus and Thrasea, second/third centuries B.C.E., in Maria Totti, *Ausgewählte Texte der Isis-und-Sarapis Religion*, Subsidia epigraphica, 12 (Hildesheim: Georg Olms, 1985), no. 1 A; Apuleius of Madaura, *Metamorphoses* 11.15.

15. Burkert, *Mystery Cults*, 41.

16. In analyzing the data for the varying ranks of female officiants in the Isis and Sarapis religion in Roman Egypt, Françoise Dunand finds that, although women were admitted to all ranks at all periods, the lower ranks of officiants in Roman Egypt seemed more heavily populated with women ("Le statut des *hiereiai* en Égypte romaine," in *Hommages à Martin Vermaseren*, vol. 1, ed. M. B. de Boer and T. A. Edridge [Leiden: E. J. Brill, 1978], 352–74). Nevertheless, it is very difficult to distinguish levels of official service, especially outside of Roman Egypt, where the inscriptional evidence suggests that Isiac priestesses of all classes were far more of a common occurrence; see Sharon Kelly Heyob, *The Cult of Isis Among Women in the Greco-Roman World*, EPRO, 51 (Leiden: E. J. Brill, 1975).

17. Heyob, *Cult of Isis*, 105.

18. See Le Corsu, *Isis*, pls. 17 and 28; Naples Museum Inv. 8919; Archaeological Museum of Palestrina, Isiac mosaic (Collection Viollet).

19. Françoise Dunand, *Religion populaire en Égypte romaine: Les terres cuites isiaques au Musée du Caire*, EPRO, 66 (Leiden: E. J. Brill, 1979).

20. Heyob, *Cult of Isis*, 14–22.

21. Tertullian, *To His Wife* 1.6; *On Chastity* 13; *On Monogamy* 17; *On Fasting* 16; Lactantius, *Divine Institutions* 1.15 (cited by Heyob, *Cult of Isis*, 110).

22. Q (for the German *Quelle,* or "source") is a hypothetical gospel consisting of a collection of Jesus' sayings; it is conjectured that it was written prior to Matthew and Luke and that those two evangelists used it, in addition to Mark, as a source. For a fuller description of the stages of this community and its "gospel," see Burton Mack, "Q and Christian Origins," in *Early Christianity, Jesus, and Q,* Semeia, 54 (Atlanta: Scholars Press, forthcoming).

23. See Elisabeth Schüssler Fiorenza, *In Memory of Her: A Feminist Theological Reconstruction of Christian Origins* (New York: Crossroad, 1983), 151ff.

24. Paula Fredriksen, *From Jesus to Christ: The Origins of the New Testament Images of Jesus* (New Haven, Conn., and London: Yale University Press, 1988), 128; Gerd Theissen, *The Sociology of Early Palestinian Christianity* (Philadelphia: Fortress Press, 1978), 8–23.

25. Cantarella, *Pandora's Daughters,* 159–66.

26. Mary R. Lefkowitz, *Women in Greek Myth* (Baltimore: Johns Hopkins University Press, 1986), 40.

27. Henri Frankfort, *Kingship and the Gods* (Chicago: University of Chicago Press, 1948), 299–301. In Jewish wisdom texts from the Hellenistic period (e.g., Wisdom of Solomon), this "royal" aspect of the Isis theology is a factor in the mythic description of Wisdom as mother and protectress of kings; see John Kloppenborg, "Isis and Sophia in the Book of Wisdom," *HTR* 75 (1982): 62.

28. See Victor Tran Tam Tinh, *Isis Lactans,* EPRO, 26 (Leiden: E. J. Brill, 1973), 4; Jean Leclant, "Le rôle d'allaîtement d'après les textes des Pyramides," *JNES* 10 (1951): 123 n. 14; see also my "The Milk of Salvation: Redemption by the Mother in Late Antiquity and Early Christianity," *HTR* 82/4 (July 1989): 393–420.

29. As related by Le Corsu, *Isis,* 8–10.

30. Theodora Hadzisteliou Price, *Kourotrophos: Cults and Representations of Greek Nursing Deities* (Leiden: E. J. Brill, 1978), 8.

31. Ibid., 202.

32. R. E. Witt, *Isis in the Greco-Roman World* (London: Thames & Hudson, 1971), 138.

33. Tran Tam Tinh, *Isis Lactans,* 7, 21.

34. Dunand, *Religion populaire;* see my "Milk of Salvation," pls. 3 and 4.

35. For the Greek text, see Totti, *Ausgewählte Texte,* no. 4; for the English translation, see F. C. Grant, *Hellenistic Religions* (New York: Liberal Arts Press, 1953), 131–33; Kraemer, *Maenads, Martyrs,* 368–70.

36. Greek text in Totti, no. 1 (1–4); English translation in Kraemer, *Maenads, Martyrs,* 367–68.

37. Heyob, *Cult of Isis,* 52–53.

38. Paul Perdrizet, *Terres cuites grecques d'Égypte de la collection Fouquet* (Paris, 1921), xx (cited in Tran Tam Tinh, *Isis Lactans,* 18).

39. Heyob, *Cult of Isis,* 79–80; Le Corsu, *Isis,* 24.

40. Heyob, *Cult of Isis,* 60; see Ladislaus Vidman, *Sylloge inscriptionum religionis Isiacae et Sarapicae* (Berlin: Walter de Gruyter, 1969), nos. 42, 97, 264, 422, 423, 424, 433, 586.

41. Heyob, *Cult of Isis,* 55.

42. Tran Tam Tinh, *Isis Lactans,* 29–30 (see *Supplementum epigraphicarum graecarum,* 8.2, 147, no. 804); see also my "Milk of Salvation," 403–4, for a fuller description of the stele.

43. See Plutarch, *On Isis and Osiris* 3; Vidman, *Sylloge,* no. 365.

44. Tran Tam Tinh, *Isis Lactans,* pl. 77, fig. 202; Price, *Kourotrophos,* fig. 26; Kraemer, *Maenads, Martyrs,* cover; my "Milk of Salvation," 404–5.

45. Tran Tam Tinh, *Isis Lactans,* 45.

46. Heyob, *Cult of Isis,* 79.

3

Model of Mediation: Wisdom and Her Children

You will wear her like a glorious robe,
and put her on like a splendid crown.
—Sirach 6:31, NRSV

The Personification of Wisdom

Wisdom (Hebrew *Hokhmah;* Greek *Sophia*)[1] was one of the most important manifestations of a saving and preserving presence in Judaism, increasingly so in the Second Temple period and especially within hellenized Judaism, which had to come to terms with the problem of a surrounding polytheistic culture. Originally, the writers of the Tanak viewed wisdom merely as an attribute of

YHWH. According to Burton Mack, Job 28 is the classic text for praise of a wisdom that is not yet personified.[2] The author of Job shares with traditional Jewish wisdom teaching the belief that wisdom, as part of the deity, pre-exists the creation of the world, and is in fact present with the deity at creation (see Prov. 8:22–31; John 1:1–4). However, from the pessimistic view of wisdom teaching that prevails in Job, divine wisdom is not accessible to anyone on earth: It is hidden even from "Abaddon and Death" (Job 28:12–22), and only YHWH understands the way to it, because only YHWH bestows it. In this text, wisdom is not a person, but an attribute, even an object or creature generated by YHWH and belonging only to YHWH and to those who have the "beginning" of wisdom, the proper "fear of YHWH." Job and his comforters, each sure in his own way that he can "find" the way to wisdom, are all wanting in those traits.

Yet it is clear that this "hidden," inaccessible, unpersonified attribute of the deity was not ultimately the most satisfying one in biblical or intertestamental Judaism. In the book of Proverbs, wisdom takes on the personification that is suggested by its grammatical gender: "It" (wisdom) becomes "she" (Wisdom). In Proverbs 3:19–20, for example, Wisdom is described in terms reminiscent at first of the hidden wisdom of Job: YHWH created the *kosmos* and its manifold operations through his own wisdom. Nevertheless, it is clear that in this text from Proverbs, Wisdom is a personage and not an attribute: "She" has hands that hold long life, riches, and honor (3:13–18). When YHWH is portrayed as creating the *kosmos* in Proverbs 8, personified Wisdom, as "the beginning of his work," is not only present at creation, but takes an active part in it, both delighting the deity as co-worker and companion, and delighting especially in the creation of humanity.

This is the Wisdom that Mack has identified as "immanent" (*nahe*), delineated both here and in the apocryphal book of Sirach 3–7: Wisdom personified as the one who is instructor, teacher, indicator of the way to YHWH and hence to life.[3] She is also the one who is the very source of life, described as the "tree of life" (Prov. 3:18; Sir. 14:26), echoing Genesis 2, and as the "water of life" (Sir. 24:25–27); she is the robe and crown that adorn and protect kings, but elevates even slaves (Sir. 6:31; 7:21).[4] Wisdom comes from YHWH and is present at the creation of the *kosmos*, but she is also *in* creation, showing those who know her and whom she "calls" the way to the divine life. In short, she is the heavenly mediator between the divine and the human realms. She also appears to have chosen this involvement out of love for humanity.

Because of this love and compassion, Wisdom is also seen as descending to earth. According to Proverbs 1:20–21 and 8:1–3, Wisdom is to be found at all places where human beings might be expected to pass by or to congregate: in the streets, in the squares of the city, at the crossroads, on the heights, beside the path, at the city gates. (The fact that these are also places where prostitutes might be encountered plays no small part in the portrayal of Wisdom and in her contrast with Folly, as will be shown below.) Wisdom calls, she invites, she accosts. She builds a house and takes up residence (Prov. 9:1–6), inviting those who would learn to live to come in. She protects those who love her in return for her love (Prov. 8:35–36), and gives them honor and prosperity. As Mack has put it, "She offers humanity life, rest, understanding, and salvation (*Heil*)."[5] In the pseudepigraphical book of *Enoch*, Wisdom descends from her heavenly home specifically to make her home in Israel (*1 Enoch* 42:2); Folly, in contrast, makes her home in the other nations (i.e., among the Gentiles, who cannot truly perceive YHWH). In the Septuagint version of the apocryphal book of Baruch, Wisdom is sent down to Israel by YHWH and is identified by Baruch with the Torah: "She is the book of the commandments of God, the law that endures forever" (Bar. 4:1, NRSV). The latter incarnation of Wisdom, meant to be an answer to the problem of theodicy inherent in the oppression of Israel at the hands of the Gentiles, is an important contribution to the male personification of Wisdom in later Judaism. Because Wisdom resides in Torah, she is also, by extension, incarnated in the persons perceived as those who embody Torah: the sages. According to Jacob Neusner, "The reason that the Torah was made flesh [i.e., in the sages] was that the Torah was the source of salvation. When the sage was transformed into a salvific figure through his mastery of the Torah, it was an easy step to regard the sage as a living Torah," and hence the personification of Wisdom.[6] In formative Judaism, the female sage or wise woman appears very rarely, and usually is later described as an adulteress or a shrew. Beruria, the wife of R. Meier, was the daughter of R. Hanania ben Teradion and stood at the stake as he was martyred by the Romans. She was revered for her knowledge of Torah and regarded as one of the Tannaim. A Beruria cycle of stories was probably composed before the fifth century C.E. It was also said of Beruria, however, that she was later seduced by one of her husband's students, proving the looseness of a learned woman.[7] Serah, the daughter of R. Asher, was supposed to have had supernatural powers of wisdom and to have kept the "secret of redemption," thus becoming immortal, but Yalta, the daughter of the president of the Babylonian Jews and wife of R. Nahman, who like Beruria argued with and chid male students and rabbis alike, was widely represented in the Babylonian Talmud as a shrew.[8] While these women continue the tradition of the wise women of ancient Israel, as we shall see, there is a tendency for the androcentric literature that describes them *not* to represent them as embodied Wisdom, but to present them as unable to be "living Torah" because of their incapacities as women. Nehama Aschkenasy regards this tendency in talmudic literature as culminating in the figure of Lilith, Adam's first wife, who refused to be instructed by him and was portrayed in legend as a child-snatching demon.[9]

However, these are all later developments. Thus far, we have shown a tendency in the biblical and extracanonical literature of Judaism, particularly in that of the Hellenistic period, when the Wisdom of Solomon and Sirach were written, to personify Wisdom, the divine attribute, as female, and to locate her not in the heavens as preexistent, but on earth with humanity, desiring it, dwelling with it, participating in it. Further, the figure of Wisdom in the Hellenistic period appears to take on certain mythic dimensions that she shares with the pagan deities of the Mediterranean world. She descends and ascends; she is a mediator between the divine and human realms; she loves, protects, and saves humanity. Like Richard Reitzenstein, Burton Mack finds many parallels between this mythology of Wisdom and the mythology of Isis. These parallels become more pronounced in the writing of Hellenistic Jewish authors like the author of the apocryphal Wisdom of Solomon, an Alexandrian Jew writing about 100 B.C.E., and Philo of Alexandria, writing at the turn of the eras.[10] Like Isis, Wisdom is concerned with justice; like Isis, who taught writing and the arts of civilization to humanity, Wisdom continues to instruct the wise in these arts, particularly in scripture; like Isis, Wisdom is concerned with the protection of kings and rulers. Wisdom, like Isis, is even seen as the savior of the righteous from the perils of this world (Wisd. Sol. 10). John Kloppenborg, moreover, has claimed that this saving aspect of the Jewish Sophia had much in common with Isis, "the savior deity of popular Greek piety," and that the author of the Wisdom of Solomon "re-mythologized" the figure of Sophia in order to "maintain [Judaism] as a saving religion," in response to the needs of hellenized Jews living in Egypt, where Isis as the center of another salvation religion may have proven a powerful rival.[11] Nevertheless, as Elisabeth Schüssler Fiorenza has pointed out, this mythic Wisdom is "strange and enigmatic" in Judaism, appearing more as a "hypostatization of an abstract concept than a real personal being," a being that is not completely realized because of the need of Judaism to avoid the "di-theism" that the personification of Wisdom would suggest.[12]

Before we consider the validity of this claim and the relationship of the literary and mythic portrayal of Wisdom to the ways actual women were seen in the periods of Judaism during which Wisdom was being personified, we should consider a unique version of Wisdom's mythologization, one that was also to figure largely in Christian representations of Jesus: that expressed by Philo of Alexandria. For Philo, who incorporated elements of Isis mythology with those of Jewish Wisdom, the female Sophia was only one aspect of the Wisdom of God. Philo, as a hellenized Jewish philosopher, was influenced by Stoicism, and from it derived his description of the more active mediating and saving form of Wisdom—that is, Wisdom's male aspect, the Logos. In *On Flight and Finding*, Philo was at some pains to point out that while the *name* of Wisdom, like that of all the virtues, was feminine, her *power* was nevertheless "manly" (*On Flight* 51–52). Because Philo's "basic orientation" is toward salvation, as Richard Baer asserts, and because it is, in true Hellenistic fashion, therefore centered upon the unity of the soul with God,[13] it might be expected that Philo's theology would have as a major focus the mediating figure between the divine and human realms, the figure of Wisdom. Although this is certainly the case, what Philo achieves in his portrayal of Wisdom is consistent with his Greek philosophical leanings: that is, he regards Wisdom in its female aspect as imperfect, passive, of a "lower order."[14] The active aspect of Wisdom, closer to the deity, described as "son" and "image," is the male Logos. Becoming like the deity—that is, becoming divine oneself—is to imitate the "singleness" of the deity, which Philo describes as becoming "virgin" and thus becoming male.[15] For Philo also, as he demonstrates in *On the Creation of the World*, the male is the image of the deity because the male portion of the self, the soul or mind

(the faculty known as *logos*), is part of the divine. The female, as represented in the creation narratives of Genesis
2–3, tempted by the pleasures of the world, represents
the irrational part of the self and, being created from
the "earthly" Adam, is doubly removed from the divine
image, representing even the lower part of the physical
being (*On the Creation of the World* 144–69; *That the Worse
Should Be Instructed by the Better* 85).

Philo's exegesis of the double creation, including his
thinking on anthropology and soteriology, was influenced not only by Stoicism, but also by Platonism, especially by Plato's *Timaeus*. The latter, together with Philo's
exegesis of it, further influenced Jewish and Christian
Gnostic thinking about the role of Sophia (Wisdom) in
the creation of the world, which the Gnostics perceived
as "fallen."[16] While we shall need to examine later the
important role of Sophia in Gnosticism, particularly as
"redeemed redeemer," it should be noted here that Philo,
like Paul (see 1 Cor. 11:2–16) and Paul's followers, interpreted the two creation stories to indicate a natural,
gendered hierarchy of being in which the female was
identified with the lower portion. It is also probably Philo
who made the identification of the male Logos as the
child of God, mediator between the human and divine
realms, bringer of rational souls to God, in preference to
the female Sophia. It was therefore natural for another
hellenized Jew, the Christian evangelist John, to envision
his descending-ascending redeemer as the male Logos.
As Philo saw the Logos incarnated in a variety of heroic
figures from Israel's past, most notably Moses, so John
easily translated the male Logos as the male Jesus who
was the divine incarnate. The depiction of the figure of
Sophia—however much it might have borrowed from the
mythic description of Isis as the ruler of the *kosmos* and the
liberator from fate and death—was not readily adapted
by either the androcentric texts of Jewish wisdom literature or the christological hymns of the New Testament.[17]
In contrast, the figure of the Logos fit with the image

of a male deity and with Hellenistic philosophical conceptions of mind and soul. Those Christians who came
from a Hellenistic Jewish philosophical bent could therefore easily identify their male savior, Christ, with the male
personification of Wisdom.

While it must remain for us later in the discussion to examine how Jesus is linked to the figure of Wisdom in the
New Testament by authors other than Paul and John, we
have seen how much more readily Wisdom was seen in
male-authored texts to be incarnated in a male, whether
he be the sage who studied Torah and himself embodied it; the personification of the rational soul on its way
toward the divine, like Moses; or the mediator between
the divine and human realms, the preexistent Logos incarnated in Jesus of Nazareth, whose resurrection was
a return to the heavenly realm whence he originated,
drawing with him all of "his own," as Wisdom had sum-
moned her children, the wise, to life. Yet we have up until
now set aside the question of whether the female personification of Wisdom, however persistently it tended to
be repersonified as male, was in any way linked to actual female persons or experiences in ancient Israel, the
intertestamental period, or the world of the New Testament. This is a question that must now be considered. In
the descriptions of Wisdom in the books of Proverbs, Sirach, and Wisdom of Solomon, the latter two particularly,
the figure of Wisdom borrows many attributes from Isis
mythology, in her portrayal as savior of nations, counselor of kings, protector of rulers, and sovereign deity
herself. However, there are also in the representation of
Wisdom, just as in the myth of Isis, many other attributes
that are more earthly and more common, those of sister,
wife, domestic manager, intimate friend or lover, even seductress. Indeed, Wisdom can elevate even the humble
to the status of rulers, so that she is not entirely confined
to the higher echelons of society. Qoheleth (Ecclesiastes),
another book of pessimistic Wisdom, like Job, states that
"Wisdom gives strength to the wise more than ten rulers

that are in a city" (Eccl. 7:19, NRSV). (This may be a pious interpolation; in any case, the overall tone of the author is misogynistic, and he makes no attempt to personify Wisdom as female.) Sirach claims that Wisdom clothes everyone who chooses her harsh discipline in royal clothing (Sir. 6:29–31) and makes even slaves equal to their masters, worthy of friendship and freedom (7:21).

Thus Wisdom is envisioned as accessible to all, from the ruler to the slave. But does this admittedly idealized literary creation intersect with the social and historical situation of women? Is there any attempt in this figure to portray a powerful female figure who, like Isis, "makes the power of women equal to that of men"? In this respect, the caveat voiced by Carol Meyers is particularly instructive: "The biblical record is a cultural document that emerges from, but does not necessarily mirror, social reality," however much it has dominated patterns of perception and behavior.[18] Nonetheless, as Claudia Camp has noted of the literary image of Wisdom in the book of Proverbs, biblical writers did have available to them a repertoire of images "associated with the idea and experience of 'woman' in Israel," although those images are of women as seen by men.[19] Hence it is true that while the image of the female cannot be directly correlated with the realities of women's experiences, it does, insofar as it is an image and therefore a metaphor, partake of those experiences in some sense, even if they are not described by women. The connection between historical women and the mythic female character Wisdom has been explored extensively by Meyers, Aschkenasy, and Camp with respect to the Hebrew Bible, and by Schüssler Fiorenza with respect to the New Testament and the role of Wisdom in the early Christian communities.[20]

For Meyers, the image of Wisdom as female relates directly to the cultural processes of ancient Israel and to women as "socializers" and preservers of the life of the community, primarily through their responsibility for the household and family stability and continuance.[21] She sees Eve, as first woman, as symbolic of all women, her connection to Wisdom being a significant one:

> The prominent role of the female rather than the male in the wisdom aspects of the Eden tale is a little-noticed feature of the narrative. It is the woman, and not the man, who perceives the desirability of procuring wisdom.... This association between the female and the qualities of wisdom may have a mythic background, with the features of the Semitic wisdom goddess underlying the intellectual prominence of the woman in Eden.... The close connection between woman and wisdom in the Bible is surely present in the creation narrative, although it is hardly limited to the beginning of Genesis. This relationship actually reaches its climax in the personification of Wisdom as a woman in Proverbs.... The Genesis text serves as preparation for what is to come in the portrayal of Woman Wisdom, of various wise women, and of women acting wisely.[22]

It is in her role as "helper" (*'ezer*), almost a benefactor, of Adam that Eve appears to be the model for Wisdom as woman and the ideal wife portrayed in Proverbs 31. Like Wisdom, the "capable wife" of Proverbs 31 manages a household (see Prov. 9:1); she is responsible for the prosperity of her husband and children. To her husband, "she does good and not harm, all the days of her life" (31:12, NRSV). Her household is actually clothed in royal clothing, just as Wisdom provides royal garments to the wise (31:21–22; see Sir. 6:31). In fact, she embodies Wisdom within her household and within the city, in which her "works" are praised: "She opens her mouth with wisdom" (31:26, NRSV).

Yet it is not only as the helper of her mate that woman is seen as behaving wisely in the Tanak. There are also a number of examples of "wise women" that are preserved in the biblical texts. Aschkenasy suggests that these wise women may have been the transmitters of Israelite culture, in that they represent the "singers of tales, those professional storytellers who transmitted their stories orally from one generation to the next, before the stories were finally committed to the written word," remnants of these tales existing in the Song of Deborah (Judg. 5) and the book of Ruth.[23] While this aspect of the activity of the wise women of Israel cannot be conclusively demonstrated, the nature of the instruction would seem to have two results, both reflected in the biblical texts. First, the wise woman's instruction is oral, and within the family it is passed down orally from mother to child. Second, this oral teaching, when written down, appears to function in the more formal "school" setting, which nonetheless is structured along the lines of the less formal family situation, as instruction delivered by the (male) master to the (male) student. The transition from familial, less formal, oral instruction to the more formal written instruction of the school serves in part to explain why, as Wisdom becomes embodied in Torah toward the end of the Hellenistic period, she loses her female character and becomes embodied in the male sage, who has already taken over the mother's less formal role as instructor.[24] We might see as a further example of this takeover how (male) Logos takes over from (female) Sophia, even though in Proverbs the role of the mother in transmitting wisdom appears to be equal to that of the father (Prov. 1:20–21; 8:1–3, 14–16; 31:13–14, 20, 24, 31). Proverbs 30–31 is the "oracle" of King Lemuel's mother, perhaps handed down orally, as was the teaching of "wise" mothers in ancient Israel.

Other wise women appear in the biblical texts as those who save not only their households but their cities or people by their advice. For this reason, the title "mother in Israel" was given certain notable women because of their "effective counsel of unity and *shalom*."[25] Among such mediators and advisers is Deborah, whose functions as judge and seer are as important to the salvation of Israel as her military abilities; it is the former functions

that gain her the title "mother in Israel" (Judg. 5:7).
Like Deborah, Abigail, wife of Nabal, saves her household
from being decimated by David, who has been incited by
her husband's folly (1 Sam. 25). Abigail appears here to
be a symbolic contrast to her husband: While his very
name means "fool" (1 Sam. 25:25), she is "clever" as
well as beautiful, and acts accordingly. Like Wisdom,
Abigail is "sent" by YHWH to prevent David from in-
curring blood-guilt because of the folly of Nabal and his
own rashness, which Abigail counters with her "good
sense." She also has the ability to see into the future: She
prophesies that David will have a "sure house."[26] Other
mediating wise women are the wise woman of Tekoa, who
persuades David to forgive and receive the banished Ab-
salom (2 Sam. 14; although the narrator claims that Joab
"put the words into her mouth"), and the wise woman of
Abel (2 Sam. 20:14–22), who persuades Joab not to destroy the city that is itself known as a "mother in Israel." It
would further appear as though the wise woman of Abel
herself, and perhaps others like her, may have gained her
city its reputation and title. As she tells Joab, "They used
to say in the old days, 'Let them inquire at Abel'; and so
they would settle a matter" (2 Sam. 20:18, NRSV). The
woman who crushes Abimelech's skull with a millstone
provides more direct defense of her city, Thebez (Judg.
9:53–54). Another woman whose advice to a king takes
a less sanctioned form is the medium of Endor (1 Sam.
28), who is sought out by Saul when all other methods
of divination fail, including dreams, prophets, and Urim
(1 Sam. 28:6). Not only does she help him to see into the
future by raising the reluctant spirit of Samuel, but she
also saves Saul's life by persuading him to eat and keep
up his strength when he is "terrified" and dispirited by
Samuel's prophecy (1 Sam. 28:22–25).

This last example may serve as a transition to another
type of wise woman in Israel: the one who exists at the
fringes of authority and uses subterfuge and subversion
to accomplish the restoration of her rights. In the story

of Judah and Tamar (Gen. 28), for example, Tamar must accomplish by indirection and seduction what is hers by right: the continuation of Judah's line through her, even though she is continually balked by male treachery, first of her brother-in-law Onan, and then of Judah himself. Aschkenasy speculates that the tale of Deborah, Jael, Sisera, and Sisera's mother, as told in Judges 5, may have "originated from a woman story-teller," with Deborah's Song originally in the first person as a form of self-praise.[27] In that tale Jael achieves her aim by subversion, her tactics providing a literary model for those of Judith, Esther, and Ruth. For Aschkenasy, as for Camp, these women are models of "tricksters and wise women," whose exclusion "from the established hierarchies of authority and power in a society obviously must lead them to utilize less direct means to achieve their goals."[28] These less direct means are related to the "paradoxical status of female sexuality," which is viewed by largely androcentric biblical texts as a sign of female weakness as well as one of female power; women's exercise of that power, when they are not under the authority of the males to whom they putatively "belong"—fathers, brothers, husbands—is perceived as threatening.[29] This view of female sexuality serves in part to explain the close parallels between the activities of the "strange woman" (*'ishsha' zara'*) as the personification of Folly in Proverbs 7:6–27 and 9:13–18, and those of the "woman of worth" (*'eshet hayil*) as the model of Wisdom in Proverbs 8–9 and 31. Wisdom plays the role of the seductress who draws her lovers to her. The young man is urged to call Wisdom his "sister" (a term typical of lovers in the ancient Near East, as attested by its frequent use in the Song of Songs) and to call insight his "intimate friend" (Prov. 7:4–5, NRSV). Just as the adulteress seeks the foolish young man "now in the street, now in the squares, at every corner" (7:12), and sits at the door of her house and at the "high places" of the town (9:14), calling to the passersby, so also does Wisdom solicit her lovers "on the heights, beside the way, at the crossroads, . . . beside the gates" (8:2–3), and at the entrance to *her* house, using the very same invitation: "You that are simple, turn in here!" (9:4, 16, NRSV).

Camp finds a parallel to this seductive sexual imagery in the Song of Songs, in which the bride also "seeks and finds" her lover, searching for him "in the streets and the city squares," being mistaken for a prostitute and wounded by the sentinels (S. of Sol. 3:2–3; 5:6–7).[30] The end or goal of this seduction is marriage, the appropriate channel for female sexuality in these texts. Improperly directed, this same powerful sexuality is described as disruptive. In the opinion of the author(s) of Proverbs, the "strange woman" ruins her marriage and her household. Not only does she forget the "partner of her youth" (Prov. 2:27), but she causes her lover to forget the wife of his own youth (5:20). The persuasive speech of the adulteress, whose words "drip honey" and are "smoother than oil" (5:3), is constantly emphasized: Like Wisdom and the wise wife, she is attractive *and* persuasive. But the man who chooses the "strange woman," who is identical with Folly, the opposite of Wisdom, chooses death, not life and health. When the young man is warned to take Wisdom for his intimate, he is urged to do so because the teacher "sees" a simple young man being seduced by the adulteress, whose "house is the way to Sheol, going down to the chambers of death" (7:27, NRSV). Wisdom's house, in contrast, is the entrance to life: When she summons her lovers to a feast, it is one of bread, meat, and wine, one that leads to health, maturity, wisdom, and ultimately to life (9:1–6). The house of the "foolish woman" plays an opposite role: It is, again, the "way to Sheol," her banquet of love nothing but bread and water, the water of death, not life.[31]

The connection of the power of both Wisdom and Folly with female sexuality provides a potent and disturbing image. One aspect of this image is that the powerful yearning of the female character for the male is a symbol of divine love that leads to eternal life. The joining of wife and husband, which leads to intimate knowledge and the creation of new life, is a model of covenant, like the joining of Israel and YHWH (see Hos. 1–3).[32] In this covenant, the wife saves her partner and her household from all the perils of life: poverty, disgrace, ill health. Like the *'eshet hayil* of Proverbs 31, she is, as the embodiment of Wisdom, "far more precious than jewels" (Prov. 31:10; see Job 28:28). In short, she is the savior of her partner. Both Camp and Meyers see this elevation of the wife to partner in postexilic Judaism as reflecting the changes in Israelite society that came about as a result of the necessity of rebuilding after the exile. During this period women's authority in the family and the household and even in the public sphere was stronger because in the face of the decentralization of authority and lack of a king, formal structures reverted to informal modes of authority.[33] But just as the mother's informal role as instructor in wisdom in the family, indeed as the embodiment of Wisdom in the house, gets taken over by the formal instruction of writing and reading in a school setting, so also the strength of the informal authority of women in Israel disappeared when authority became concentrated in the hands of the priests who reinstituted the Law and of the sages who studied it. Ezra the scribe's restoration of the priesthood after the exile (586–538 B.C.E.) and the scribal movement that followed it were thus inimical to seeing Wisdom in her domestic and maternal incarnation. The other disturbing aspect of the link between female sexuality and Wisdom is the very domestication (and therefore channeling) of that sexuality. When female Wisdom takes on a male partner (usually as husband), he is the proper direction of her care. Even Wisdom as the "consort" of kings in the Wisdom of Solomon is a manifestation of this role. Just as undomesticated female sexuality is disruptive and destructive, so also the undomesticated form of Wisdom is Folly, whose actions are described as disruptive and destructive of primarily male life and of the household.

Children and Messengers of Wisdom

The divine attribute of Wisdom that became personified as female in Jewish wisdom teaching increasingly was made to serve androcentric interests, beginning with her incarnation as the written Torah and subsequently as the dual Torah, embodied in its students and teachers, the male sages. However, she is also the mother of two "daughters," two manifestations of Wisdom that represent transformations of the Wisdom figure in the early Christian period: (1) the Sophia of the communities represented in the New Testament by Matthew's and Luke's adaptations of the Q source and by the christological hymns found in John 1:1–18, Philippians 2:6–11, Colossians 1:15–20, and Hebrews 1:1–14; outside the New Testament this Sophia is represented in the *Gospel of Thomas;* and (2) the Sophia in her various guises in Gnosticism. Like their mother, both "daughters" of the Jewish Sophia are eventually overshadowed by male incarnations, especially in the New Testament and in Christian Gnosticism related to it, which replaces Sophia with the male Logos, Jesus.

The Sophia found in the Q community is related to the "sayings traditions" of Jesus, represented in the New Testament by the Gospels of Matthew and Luke. In these, Jesus, who originally was perceived as Wisdom's envoy, became, especially in Matthew, the very incarnation of Wisdom herself.[34] According to Schüssler Fiorenza, the "Sophia-God" of the communities that produced Q, who is honored by her children and proclaimed by her messenger (Jesus), is an image that supports the discipleship of equals and the equality of women as disciples: "Sophia, the God of Jesus, wills the wholeness and humanity of everyone and therefore enables the Jesus movement to become a 'discipleship of equals.' "[35] It is this Sophia, "the Wisdom of God," who sends John the Baptist and Jesus out as her emissaries, as she sent the prophets in the past and as she continues to send her messengers, the apostles (Luke 11:49–51; Q 11:49–52). It is this Sophia who mourns over Jerusalem, longing to gather her children under her protective wings (Luke 13:34–35; Q 13:34–35). Nevertheless, although this image of Sophia embodies the care of a mother for her children, the practice of discipleship of the Jesus movement intensely rejected domestic life, the family, and the household. Hence the mother of the household, the Wisdom of the home, as she is visualized in Proverbs, is necessarily rejected as an incarnation of Sophia, even as is demonstrated in the (non-Q) Lukan story of Martha (the householder) and Mary (the wise man's disciple). What Wisdom there is in Martha and Mary's home in Bethany is being communicated by Jesus, the male instructor (Luke 10:38–42). Mary's choice of the "good part" is to abandon that home and its instruction for the life of following the wandering teacher. This is the pattern that appears to be followed by the women of the Christian communities familiar to Luke: an itinerancy that supported the proclamation of "the good news of the kingdom of God" throughout "cities and villages" (Luke 8:1–3, NRSV).

That this behavior—the rejection of contemporary social roles—was characteristic of the Q community has been demonstrated by John Kloppenborg and Burton Mack.[36] How this involves Sophia and her relationship to the women of the Jesus movement is somewhat problematic, for as Hal Taussig has pointed out, the seven specific references to women in the Q material characterize them as domestic, child-rearing, and encumbered by family; whereas Sophia herself is "remarkably domestic," the householder and mother looking after her children, just as she is portrayed in Proverbs.[37] An apparent rejection of this way of looking at Sophia and her daughters emerges in the conflict arising between the Q community and its surrounding institutions. Q then envisions a different mythic aspect of Sophia: She is publicly scorned and rejected, especially by the centers of formal instruction, the Temple and the synagogues. As Mack sees it, this conflict between the members of the Q community, especially at its third level of development, and the familial and religious institutions of their society led to a "mythologization" of Sophia as the one who is eternally rejected by Israel, even as her children and envoys are rejected (Luke 11:49–51). Ironically, however, this mythologizing of Sophia led to her role being taken over by the one who had, in the earliest stratum of Q, been seen as her child—Jesus. Hence, for the Q community in its final transformation, "Jesus came to be seen as an imposing figure of divine wisdom and will."[38] The rejection of Sophia, the caring maternal deity, became the rejection of Jesus, her child and envoy, who called down eschatological judgment upon those who rejected his teaching. As an example of this transformation, consider the differences between the saying on the rejection of Sophia in Luke 11:49–51, which probably preserves the original Q form, and in Matthew 23:34–36. Whereas the Lukan recension clearly has the "Wisdom [Sophia] of God" tell the Pharisees and scribes, "I will send them prophets and apostles, some of whom they will kill and persecute," the Matthean version has equally clearly changed the speaker to Jesus himself, and the messengers include "sages and scribes," reflecting the Matthean debate against the interpretation of the Torah that rejects Jesus as messiah. It is thus the teaching of the messiah Jesus, which embodies Sophia, that is rejected, and not Sophia herself. In the *Gospel of Thomas*, which is a Gnostic Christian sayings gospel, the transformation of Sophia into Jesus is complete. In *Thomas*, Jesus speaks as Sophia come into the world: "I stood in the midst of the world, and I appeared to them in the flesh; I found all of them drunken; I found none of them athirst. And my soul was afflicted for the children of humanity" (*Gospel of Thomas 28*).[39]

With the Jesus-Sophia of *Thomas*, we are moving toward still another transformation of Sophia in the New Testament, related to the Q traditions, but one that is more fully developed in the "mythic" tradition of Wisdom as represented by Philo of Alexandria and the Gnostics. As Helmut Koester has observed, "The full-fledged application of the wisdom myth to Jesus supersedes the more limited view of Jesus as Wisdom's envoy."[40] This "mythic" representation of Jesus appears in the christological hymns of the New Testament in the figure of the descending-ascending savior, found in its oldest form in Philippians 2:6–11, but in its fullest form as the Logos in the Gospel of John.[41] In John, Jesus is the preexistent Logos, who is identical with God. This Logos is present, like Sophia, at creation and in creation. Indeed, like Sophia, Jesus-Logos descends to Israel—"his own"— and, like Sophia, is rejected by those who do not "know" him (see *1 Enoch* 42). The heavenly Logos, like the heavenly Sophia, is a mediator between the divine and human realms: He comes into the world to give those who do receive him "the power to become the children of God" (John 1:10–12). Recognition and acceptance of the heavenly Logos give these "children" eternal life (3:36; 5:25), whereas rejection by those who fail to see, know, and accept the divine Logos in the world (5:39) brings them darkness (which is the darkness of their folly) and death. Salvation is recognition of Jesus' true identity, which also provides the believer's own: By recognizing and thereby receiving Jesus as heavenly Wisdom come to earth, one attains an identity that is like that of Jesus; one becomes a child of God. However, as James M. Robinson has cogently argued, the presentation of Jesus as heavenly Wisdom, the masculine Christ as the male Logos, overwhelmed the concept of Jesus as the envoy and child of a maternal heavenly Wisdom and indeed obscured maternal terminology in Christian doctrine: "The survival of

Wisdom in the top echelon of deity would have assured
a female part at the top (which may be part of the reason
that Wisdom was dropped [in Christian theology and so-
teriology]). Wisdom was fading fast by the time the New
Testament itself was written."[42] Paul, to whom Christ as
the descending-ascending savior was a particularly important image, says flatly in an indictment of the "wisdom
of the world" that "Christ is the Wisdom [Sophia] of God"
(1 Cor. 1:24).

Not only was Wisdom herself fading fast, but female
representatives of Wisdom were also obscured in the
New Testament. The Corinthian prophetesses, who apparently believed that they received the wisdom and
power of God from their ecstatic experiences, were urged
by Paul to obscure themselves by veils and observe
"proper" decorum for women (1 Cor. 11:2–16). Mary,
Jesus' mother, who appears in Luke's Gospel more than
in any other, especially in the infancy narratives (Luke
1:1–2:52), is not Jesus' instructor in wisdom, as might
be expected of the mother of the household and one so
important to the redemption of Israel and the Gentiles.
Instead, it is the adolescent Jesus who instructs both the
sages in the Temple and his own parents, who do not
understand his saying about being in "his Father's house"
(2:41–52). He appears to develop in wisdom without any
assistance from his mother or any sage (2:39, 52). Mary
of Bethany as a pupil studying with the sage Jesus has already been mentioned (10:38–42), but Martha, her sister,
plays little role in the Synoptic Gospels, although both
have a greater role in John. A similar obscurity is the
fate of Mary Magdalene and the other women mentioned
as disciples by Luke in 8:1–3. In Acts, where women,
including Jesus' mother, are represented as being at Pen-
tecost, at which the Spirit is poured upon "both men and
women," they do not appear in prominent roles in the
rest of the book, and it is the seven men chosen to help
the twelve who are described as "full of the Spirit and
of Wisdom" (Acts 6:3). It is only in the Gospel of John

that women appear to have a more prominent role as dialogue partners and witnesses (the Samaritan woman [John 4]; Martha of Bethany [John 11]; Mary Magdalene [John 20:1–19]). Nevertheless, they, like John the Baptist, are not meant to embody wisdom themselves, but to "bear testimony" to the one who is both Wisdom and instructor, the revealer of truth.

Sophia: The Saved Savior

In order to see better the traditions and the images from which the formers of the biblical canon selected, it is often helpful to look at the repositories of images that they did *not* select, those extracanonical materials that are now fortunately available to us. Of particular relevance to the representation of Jesus Christ as saving Wisdom in the New Testament are the Gnostic texts represented in the Nag Hammadi library, many of which were produced by Gnostic Christians, for whom saving Wisdom had a special, even central, significance. Recognition of Wisdom in the world, however the world attempts to obscure it, is the criterion for salvation in Gnosticism, with which both the Wisdom traditions represented by Q and John intersect. The Gnostic Sophia, who plays a central role in Gnostic myth, combines the features of traditional Jewish Wisdom and her obverse, Folly, the spiritual and the physical. Although the figure of Sophia is heavily mythologized in the Gnostic texts and has many variants, she does share with the traditional Jewish Wisdom the following characteristics as a savior and mediator between the divine and human realms:[43] She comes from the heavenly realm; she descends, in

some form, to earth; and she is responsible for the ultimate salvation of humanity, or at least some of humanity,
through the imparting of knowledge (*gnosis* or *sophia*),
which is also "acquaintance" with God. In short, we might
see her as incarnated in humans, at least insofar as their
spirit, through heeding Wisdom's teaching, is capable of
being awakened to its true "home" and destiny: the spiritual realm. This is the salvation that belongs to Gnostic
thinking: the knowledge that the true self is spiritual,
partaking not of this earth, but of the "realm above," all
of which radiates outward from a single divine element,
variously referred to as the All, the One, the Mother-
Father, the Fullness. Sophia is part of that realm that is
the one closest to earth and human life on it. As in the
traditional Jewish Wisdom myth, Sophia moves between
the divine and human realms, joining the two into one,
calling her "own" (the wise, the enlightened) out of the
world, making them "children of God," and giving them
eternal—that is to say, spiritual—life.

Nevertheless, the involvement of Sophia with the world
and with humanity, as presented in the Gnostic literature,
is a paradox, just as her nature is represented paradoxically. On the one hand, Sophia and her manifestations
(Ennoia, Pronoia, Epinoia, Zoe, Pistis, Eve, Norea) are
responsible for the enlightenment (*gnosis*) that leads to
salvation, the knowledge that human beings truly are the
"children of God" because they have a heavenly origin.
On the other hand, Sophia and her female hypostases
would not have had to become involved with the enlightenment of humankind had it not been for Sophia's
prior involvement in creation, the creation of the physical
world, which is perceived by Gnostics as tragic. Because
of her illegitimate desire to "create" on her own, she gen-
erates a monstrous offspring, usually called Yaldabaoth,
the deity who actually creates the physical and material universe. This offspring is defective because Sophia
herself is incomplete: She either has no male consort or
counterpart to perfect the offspring, or she fails to ask for

consent from the divine Mother-Father before she creates. As was nearly universally believed in late antiquity,
the female part in procreation was passive, inadequate,
incomplete. That is why, in most of the Gnostic versions
of the Sophia myth, particularly the Christianized ones,
Sophia is spoken of as having a "lack" or "deficiency,"
which must be remedied by her completion through a
male consort or by her acting like a male.[44] Her role
as mother, therefore, far from preserving the life of her
partner or her children, as did the Wisdom of Proverbs,
may in fact vitiate her role as savior. In most of the Gnostic texts, the creation of matter—especially of flesh and
the act of sexual intercourse, which takes place between
and reproduces physical bodies—is negative and is particularly linked with the exercise of female sexuality and
motherhood. Thus the "works of the female" are allied
with physicality and imperfection, lead to destruction instead of salvation, and must ultimately be redeemed by
"maleness," often represented as virginity, which symbolizes wholeness. For example, the creation myth in
the Gnostic tractate *On the Origin of the World* relates the
following:

[The man followed] the earth,
The woman followed [the man],
And marriage followed the woman,
And reproduction followed marriage,
And death followed reproduction.
(*Origin of the World* 109.22–26)[45]

Like the multiform figure of Sophia herself, however,
the relationship of Sophia to being female (and what "female" means), to being mother, and to being savior in
Gnostic texts, Christian and non-Christian, is expressed
in diverse and often contradictory ways. As Michael A.
Williams notes of the variety of Gnostic perspectives on
gender:

We must...distinguish between the question of how much gendered imagery appears in a text and the question of how much the author is really interested in the gender of the images. An even further distinction must be made between an author's interest in the gendered character of the images and the relation of the gender roles depicted to patterns of socialization that are preferred or advocated.[46]

In the *Trimorphic Protennoia* (*First Thought in Three Forms*), for example, Sophia has three forms, Father, Mother, and Son (Logos) (*First Thought* 38.2–16), and "descends," as did the classic Jewish figure of Sophia, to illumine, and therefore to save, "her own" in the world. In *Thunder, Perfect Mind,* and in other Gnostic tractates—for example, the *Apocryphon of John,* the *Second Stele of Seth,* and the *Second Treatise of the Great Seth*—Sophia is regarded "as the preeminent female aeon in the divine realm."[47] In *Thunder, Perfect Mind,* the speaker (Sophia) describes herself in a litany of praise and self-revelation through a series of paradoxes, which include a number of female roles that are directly contrasted:

> I am she who is honored and she who is disgraced.
> I am the harlot and the holy one.
> I am the woman and the maiden.
> I am [the mother] and the daughter.
>
> I am the members of my mother.
> I am the barren one and many are her children.
> I am she whose wedding(s) are many, and I have not
>   married.
> I am the midwife and she who does not deliver.
> I am the solace of my labor pains.
>   (*Thunder* 13.15–25)[48]

This series of paradoxes might well describe a divine figure who, like Isis, embraces the opposites. Like Wisdom

in the intertestamental literature and in the Q community, she is "sent from the power," but is "cast out upon the
earth," scorned, and despised (13.2; 14.34; 15.31), as are
her messengers (18.15). She is "the Sophia of the Greeks
and the Gnosis of the barbarians" (16.3–4), and is also
identified with Isis: "I am she whose images are many in
Egypt" (16.7). Thunder, therefore, is a manifestation of
Wisdom in many different mythic guises, most of which
appear to be female. However, she is also androgynous:
"I am the bride and the bridegroom" (13.27).

Androgyny and/or syzygy (union of opposites) also
plays a role in descriptions of Sophia in Gnosticism. Even
in the *Trimorphic Protennoia,* the divine aspect who ascends
for the second time "in the likeness of a female" (Sophia)
is described as androgynous: "[I am both Mother and]
Father since [I copulated] with myself" (45.2–11). Since
it is androgynous, this form of copulation is preferred
and is itself a form of salvation: Sophia the Mother-Father
also copulates with those who love her. Androgyny is
the original state of perfection of humanity, particularly
for those Gnostics who followed the teaching of Valentinus, a Christian Gnostic. In the Valentinian *Gospel of
Philip*, Sophia is divided into "higher" and "lower." In
her "higher" form she is the partner of the savior in the
heavenly realm of the Eight (Ogdoad). She is referred to
as "salt" (59.25–35) and is invoked by the apostles to become their "partner."[49] Throughout the *Gospel of Philip*,
images of union as salvation—the recovery of an original androgynous existence through the sacrament of
the "bridal chamber"—are paramount. In *Eugnostos the
Blessed*—a non-Christian Gnostic epistle that appeared in
a later Christianized form as the *Sophia of Jesus Christ*—the
figure of Sophia appears as unambiguously androgynous
in the syzygy Sophia/Anthropos (Sophia/Primal Human).
But, in subsequent versions of this text, as demonstrated
by Deirdre A. Good, the androgyny of Sophia cannot be
sustained: She first becomes "consort" of Anthropos, then
is separated from her consort, enabling her independent

generative activity in creation to be "translated" in the Christian version of the text into her being "at fault," and therefore needing the remedy of salvation.[50] Further, the androgynous character of Sophia, like the "image of the androgyne" in early Christian and Gnostic Christian circles, could not be sustained.[51]

In many of the Gnostic texts, the figure of Sophia, as female, is split into various roles, some of which are salvific, others of which are in need of saving. She has three main roles: that of the offspring or daughter of the deity, created through a spiritual emanation; that of the mother; and that of the consort, partner, or helper. The obverse of all three is the whore or prostitute. As the disobedient offspring, Sophia appears to take on the role assigned in intertestamental Jewish and early Christian exegesis to Eve. In Gnostic exegesis of the Genesis creation narrative, Eve is a positive character because she is the first to desire wisdom, which makes humankind divine. This desire of a disobedient Sophia is not to gain wisdom, but to create without aid or consent. In the Valentinian *Letter of Peter to Philip,* the risen Christ explains that the "powers of the world," which are "deficient" and therefore evil, are the result of the "disobedience and foolishness of the mother" (e.g., Sophia) and of her arrogance in wishing to emanate something without the consent of the Father of the All (*Letter of Peter to Philip* 135.10–20). In *The Interpretation of Knowledge,* the savior tells his disciples that "the flesh [is] an aeon that Wisdom has projected" (12.30–34). Therefore, Sophia needs to repent: Her action in fact makes Wisdom into Folly, which in traditional wisdom teaching had always been the reverse of Wisdom. It is in this sense that she takes on the role of the prostitute, the whore, "Sophia Prounikos" (Vulgar Wisdom). In the *Second Treatise of the Great Seth,* the savior explains that the "bodily dwellings" in which human beings appear to be trapped are the creation of Sophia: "For those who were in the world had been prepared by the will of our sister Sophia—she who is a whore" (50.26–29). Thus

Sophia is responsible for the "Fall"—a fall into the "works of femaleness," into the chaos of sexuality and fleshly reproduction from which the material realm is made. It is this fall that must be redeemed.

The role of Wisdom in Proverbs as the wise mother—the sustainer and counselor of her household, her children, and her spouse—has been preserved but made problematic in many of the Gnostic texts. On the one hand, the Gnostic Sophia, like her progenitress in Proverbs, is a "tree of life," who brings life into being and also sustains it. As Aydeet Fischer-Mueller has pointed out, the Gnostic Sophia, as a mythic figure, links the perfect spiritual realm (which is true life) with the imperfect physical realm through two aspects of her "motherhood."[52] This myth is told in its fullest version in the *Apocryphon of John.* As the spiritual mother, Sophia merges with Epinoia (Afterthought) and Eve (Zoe) to redeem Adam from the sleep of ignorance, and thus becomes truly "mother of the living." On the other hand, Sophia's actual motherhood, in the sense of producing offspring, is deficient and terrible, as embodied in Yaldabaoth, the evil creator of the physical *kosmos.* Thus, according to Fischer-Mueller, Sophia's activity as savior reduces her as female, since she must repent her desire to create: Saving activity, in the *Apocryphon of John,* is that of the male.[53] This portrait of a Wisdom divided into two parts, one the active and male, linked to the spiritual realm and therefore closer to the divine, and the other the passive and female, linked to the physical realm and the passions, is also found in Philo's *On the Creation of the World.*

In other Gnostic transformations, especially those described by the disciples of the teacher Valentinus, Sophia as mother is divided into a "higher" and a "lower" form, just as Wisdom's opposite in Proverbs, Folly, had many of her same characteristics.[54] The higher Wisdom, Sophia, is designated "the Mother," whereas the lower, disobedient Wisdom is "Sophia Prounikos," the "Vulgar" or the "Whore." She is also described as Echmoth, a variant of

Hokhmah, the Hebrew Wisdom, but is defined as "the Sophia of death" (*Gospel of Philip* 60.10–15). Just as Wisdom in Proverbs, represented by the *'eshet hayil*, had her obverse in the figure of Folly, represented by the adulteress, so higher Sophia, connected with the spiritual realm, has as her obverse the lower Sophia, connected with the material. This lower Sophia is further flawed because she is "female from a female" (*1 Apocalypse of James* 34.3–4). Because she lives just outside the heavenly (spiritual) realm, she is bound to become involved with material creation, and therefore with death, the decay of the material. In these versions of the Gnostic Sophia myth, it is the lower Sophia's desire to create that results in the formation of Yaldabaoth, a creature that is described as a "miscarriage," an "abortion," and is linked especially and solely to female sexuality, a sexuality that is unruly and that causes separation from the male. This separation results in imperfection because the formative ("male") element is missing, because there is only flesh without spirit. Further, the separation results in mere physicality. Therefore those who would be "perfect" must be "male" in the sense that they are oriented toward the spiritual rather than the physical (see *Zostrianos* 131.6–8). Some highly ascetic Christian Gnostic texts, like *The Book of Thomas the Contender,* are more specific: "Woe to you who love intimacy with womankind and polluted intercourse with it!" (114.9–10).[55] In the *Second Treatise of the Great Seth,* the savior (Christ, whose "image" is Jesus) takes over the mediating role of Sophia and urges, "Do not become female, lest you give birth to evil and its brothers" (65.25–26).[56]

Nevertheless, there are other "spiritual" children of Sophia. Some are sent by her into the world to redeem that part of her spiritual essence that has "fallen" into the world. Others are represented as hypostases of her. In the *Apocryphon of John,* Sophia's repentance for her folly enables her to redeem it by sending the Epinoia (Afterthought) of Light to Adam, whose body is a "dead" thing shaped by the ruler of the world, yet breathing a heavenly spirit. This hypostasis speaks as Eve (Life or Zoe) to illumine Adam and to correct Sophia's "fault." The savior tells John, "Now, Wisdom (Sophia) our sibling, who innocently descended in order to rectify her lack, was therefore called life (Zoe) [= Eve]—i.e., mother of the living—by the forethought [Pronoia] of the absolute power of heaven. . . . And thanks to it [i.e., her, Zoe] they [the illumined] tasted perfect acquaintance [*gnosis*]" (*Apocryphon of John* 23.20–25).[57] In the *Hypostasis of the Archons*, several "daughters" or female emissaries of Sophia help to save Adam, bound as he is in the body, from the sleep of ignorance caused by Yaldabaoth. The first is a "spirit-endowed Woman" who appears as the spiritual Eve, recognized by Adam as both his consort and his redeemer: "It is you who have given me life; you will be called 'mother of the living.' For it is she who is my mother. It is she who is the midwife [alt. trans., 'physician'], and the woman, and she who has given birth" (*Hypostasis* 89.11–18).[58] She also appears as the Female Spiritual Principle, who encourages the primal couple to eat of the fruit of the life-giving tree of *gnosis*. She reappears "from the world above" as the undefiled virgin Norea, the offspring of Eve and Adam. She plays a leading role as helper and savior of humanity, herself having been saved from defilement by the earthly powers, whom she chides by her wisdom when they teach her that they have defiled the "true" (spiritual) Eve, her mother, instead of her physical body. Anne McGuire even suggests that Norea, like other wise women whom we have seen, uses subversion to combat the "oppressive powers that illegitimately claim the cosmos, the social order, the psyche, and the body."[59] Other daughters or hypostases of Sophia appear as instructors in wisdom; their instruction, like the teaching of the mothers of Israel, is oral and at times visionary. In the fragmentary treatise *Hypsiphrone*, the character of Hypsiphrone, the virgin "High Mind," descends into the world to communicate saving

knowledge. In *Allogenes,* the female guide, Youel, is the
spiritual revealer of the divine powers to Allogenes. In
the *Hypostasis of the Archons* and in *On the Origin of the
World,* Zoe (Life), the daughter of Sophia, first rebukes
the arrogance of Yaldabaoth, and is the instructress of
Yaldabaoth's repentant offspring, Sabaoth. In the latter
work, Zoe and Sabaoth, now her "consort," create seven
good powers, who are androgynous. In *On the Origin of
the World,* Eve is the daughter of Zoe and is a "redeemed
redeemer" in that she, the first virgin, heals herself and
instructs Adam, uttering a hymn of self-praise that is reminiscent of the paradoxical aretalogy in *Thunder, Perfect
Mind:*

> I am the portion of my mother,
>   and I am the mother.
> I am the woman,
>   and I am the virgin.
> I am the pregnant one.
> I am the physician,
> I am the midwife.
> My husband is the one who begot me,
>   and I am his mother.
>   (*Origin* 114.9–15)[60]

Thus we can see that in the sense of purely spiritual motherhood, Sophia still plays a role in salvation, as do her
spiritual daughters. They continue her role as instructress in the wisdom that leads to spiritual (and therefore
eternal) life.

But if Sophia is a mother, she is also a consort: Who is
the true consort of Sophia? The answer varies, depend-
ing on the variety of Gnosticism represented. In texts
of Sethian Gnosticism, as Pearson notes, the soteriolog-
ical function is shared between the female and the male
partners of a syzygy, but the secondary Christianization
of such texts resulted in the "masculinization of Gnostic soteriology," the role of Epinoia, for example, being

taken over by Christ in the *Apocryphon of John* and by the True Man (who is also Christ) predicted by Eleleth to Norea in *Hypostasis of the Archons*. Further, Sophia is replaced by Immortal Anthropos (Christ) in *Sophia of Jesus Christ*.[61] The extreme of this masculinization occurs in the *Tripartite Tractate*, where the author models the myth of the descending, self-redeemed, and ascending male Logos upon that of the female Sophia. The Logos becomes "Son," "Bride," "Savior, Redeemer, and Christ" (*Tripartite Tractate* 87.5) after his repentance at the creation of the visible world, and his rejection of the "illness which is femaleness" and weakness (94.15).[62] The same masculinization of Sophia occurs in some Valentinian Gnostic texts. In the *Gospel of Truth*, for example, said to have been written by Valentinus himself, the redemptive Logos (Christ), who comes from the Father, brings the errant "All" back "into the Father, into the Mother, Jesus of the infinite gentleness" (24.5).[63] According to Hippolytus's version of the Valentinian myth of Sophia, which Hippolytus explains in *Refutation of All Heresies* (6.31.5–6), the "lower" Sophia takes Jesus, the earthly or "psychic" aspect of the heavenly Christ, as her spouse, in order to "correct" the passions she engendered as she suffered for the results of her solitary creation. In the *Dialogue of the Savior*, the Logos (savior) emanates directly from the father and comes to "destroy the works of femaleness" (*Dialogue* 144.20–21).[64] In *1 Apocalypse of James*, in which the lower Sophia, Achamoth, is responsible for the creation of the world, the higher Sophia resides "in the Father" and is represented by the savior, "the imperishable Sophia."[65] In the non-Gnostic Christian wisdom text in the Nag Hammadi Library, *The Teachings of Silvanus*, Christ is both Logos and Sophia: "For the Tree of Life is Christ. He is Wisdom. For He is Wisdom; He is also the Word" (*Silvanus* 106.21–24).[66]

This latter role of Sophia as spouse, especially as represented in Christian Gnostic texts, leads us to ask whether the Gnostic Sophia can be truly regarded as a savior figure, and in what ways. As we have seen, she sends her wisdom into the world (a world for which her "error" is responsible), in various spiritual representations, to bring humanity back to its true origin, the godhead. In this sense, she performs the saving role of traditional Wisdom, who brings the wise, her lovers and children, to God. But in the Gnostic version of the Wisdom myth, Sophia must first repent her error—her desire to create without a male partner and without the consent of her "parent"—and "correct her deficiency." This error is often portrayed as adultery or prostitution and becomes a pattern for the fall and redemption of the soul itself, which is also represented as female. Hence the primal transgression is once again, as in the canonical texts, represented by the perceived "misuse" or misdirection of female sexuality: A female figure acts on her own, without proper consent and without an appropriate partner. Sophia's restoration thus is frequently expressed as a union (syzygy) with a male partner. In *A Valentinian Exposition,* Sophia "suffers" from the passions created after she separates from her syzygy, and repents: "Granted that I have [left] my consort. Therefore [I am] beyond confirmation as well. I deserve the things I suffer" (34.25–30).[67] When reunited with her consort, Jesus, she is redeemed and reconciled to the heavenly Pleroma (Fullness), her origin. In the same text, Sophia represents the church in the syzygy of Anthropos (Christ) and church (31.35). In the Sethian *Holy Book of the Great Invisible Spirit,* Sophia is not represented at all in the higher realms, but only in the material, or hylic, realm, where her repentance becomes personified as Metanoia, who causes the heavenly redeemer, Seth, to be sent. He "puts on" the garment of Jesus in order to save his children in the world. The second descent of the *Trimorphic Protennoia,* "in the likeness of a female," redeems the lower Sophia, "the guileless one," but even this descent is also described as androgynous, while the third and final descent is that of the Son, the Logos, the male offspring who "puts on" Jesus. Thus it would appear that most Gnostic representations of Sophia as redeemed redeemer, the model of and for the human soul, require her to be united with a male counterpart, who in the Christian Gnostic versions takes over her redemptive activities. "Christ," her spiritual male counterpart, becomes not only Wisdom but spiritual mother.

Although Christ himself becomes the embodiment of Sophia, women disciples function as spiritual instructors in the Gnostic texts, sometimes as instructors of even higher wisdom than the men. In the *1 Apocalypse of James*, in which the sufferings of the world are caused by the lower Sophia, who is "female from a female," seven women are nevertheless said to be Jesus' disciples, of whom three are mentioned: Mariam, Martha, and Arsinoe (38.15–20). In the *Gospel of Philip*, three women are mentioned as being "companions" of Jesus: "There were three who always walked with the Lord: Mary his mother and her sister and Magdalene, the one who was called his companion. His sister and his mother and his companion were each a Mary" (59.5–15).[68] This gospel reveres the syzygy—the union of the soul and its "angel" that occurs in the spiritual "bridal chamber"—as it re-creates the original androgynous nature of humanity. The "companion," Mary Magdalene, appears herself in syzygy with Christ, just as the heavenly Sophia is often represented as the companion of the heavenly Logos or spiritual Christ. Certainly the gospel gives Mary an important role as one who has complete unity with Christ. According to the *Gospel of Philip* (63.30–64.10), the other disciples are jealous of the savior's intimacy with his companion, as he "[used to] kiss her [often] on her [mouth]," a sign of spiritual unity or perhaps of the intimate transmission of secret teaching. When the other disciples express disapproval, saying, "Why do you love her more than all of us?" Jesus replies enigmatically with a parable on illumination: "Why do I not love you like her? When one who is blind and one who

sees are both together in darkness, they are no different from one another. When the light comes, then the
one who sees will see the light, and the one who is blind
will remain in darkness."[69] Apparently Mary sees the
light of the savior and his teaching more clearly than the
others.

Mary continues to play a leading part as an instructor,
revealer, and wise woman in other Gnostic texts: In the
Dialogue of the Savior, according to Elaine Pagels, she appears as a "symbol of divine Wisdom."[70] Although in the
same highly ascetic dialogue the savior Jesus tells the disciples to "pray in the place where there is no woman"
and to "destroy the works of femaleness" (144.15–25),
nevertheless Mary (Mariam) is one of the three disciples
who are his dialogue partners. It is Mary who interprets
three of Jesus' sayings known from the Synoptic Gospels,
on the day's evil being sufficient to the day, the labor-
ers being worthy of their hire, and the resemblance of
disciple and teacher: "This word she spoke as a woman
who knew the All" (139.10).[71] Thus Mary shows her superior knowledge of the divine. She is even the revealer
of her own gospel, *The Gospel of Mary,* which is typical of
a Gnostic gospel in that it is a revelation dialogue. But
once again, the jealousy of the other male disciples in-
tervenes: First Andrew questions the "strange ideas" that
Mary has taught them from the savior; then Peter questions, "Did he really speak privately with a woman (and)
not openly to us? Are we to turn about and all listen
to her? Did he prefer her to us?" Levi chides Peter for
speaking "against the woman like the adversaries. But if
the Savior made her worthy, who are you indeed to reject
her? Surely the Savior knew her very well. That is why
he loved her more than us" (17.5–18.20).[72] Mary's teaching is also challenged in the *Pistis Sophia* (Faith-Wisdom)
(36.71), although she is "superior to all the disciples"
(17.97), and in the *Gospel of Thomas* (51.19–26), perhaps
the best-known instance of the antagonism between Peter
and Mary:

Simon Peter said to them: "Let Mary leave us, for women are not worthy of [the] Life." Jesus said, "I myself shall lead her, in order to make her male, so that she too may become a living spirit, resembling you males. For every woman who will make herself male will enter the Kingdom of Heaven."[73]

What are we to make of these instances and sayings? On one level, the antagonism toward Mary and her teaching on the part of Peter, the "chief of the apostles" in orthodox Christian circles, may represent antagonism toward women's leadership in Gnostic and heterodox Christianity.[74] The Montanist prophetess Maximilla,[75] for example, claimed to be "Word and Spirit and Power" (Eusebius, *Ecclesiastical History* 5.16, 17), while Helen, the companion of the Gnostic teacher Simon, represented the fallen and redeemed Sophia (Irenaeus, *Against Heresies* 1.23.2). Irenaeus inveighed against the "many foolish women" who were "seduced" by the Gnostic teacher Marcus, who taught them to invoke the female Gnostic powers, Grace (Charis), "She who is before all things," Wisdom (Sophia), and Silence (Sige) (*Against Heresies* 1.13.3–5). Tertullian, who in his pre-Montanist phase was against the leadership of women in North African Christian congregations, hardened the Pauline line and forbade women to teach or assume any "masculine" office or function. He does that in the same letter in which he condemns women as "Eve," the "gateway of the devil, the traitor of the tree" (*On the Adornment of Women* 1.1).

But these texts represent more than simple antagonism against women's formal teaching, especially of men. As has previously been noted, maleness in Gnostic teaching, as for religious, philosophical, and medical thinking in Greco-Roman antiquity, usually stood for completion and for spirituality. The female without the male was incomplete, as shown mythically by Sophia's incomplete, abortive creation, which cannot make anything truly good. However, the divisions between maleness and

femaleness in the Gnostic texts are not always so neat.
In a passage from the *Gospel of Thomas*, for example,
Jesus is going to "lead" or "attract" Mary, in order that
she may not stand on her own as a female, but become
part of the androgynous syzygy of which he is the male
part. Perfection, then, is not simply maleness by itself. As
Levi reminds Peter in the *Gospel of Philip*, to "put on the
perfect man" is not to reject Mary and her teaching, because in a sense she has already put on the "perfect man"
by her intimacy with the savior.[76] This "putting on" has
echoes of Paul's advice in Galatians 3:27–28, in which all
Christians, regardless of gender, have "put on" Christ.
Nonetheless, it is also clear that the female part of the androgynous syzygy is not equal to the male part, just as the
unveiled charismatic women of Paul's Corinthian congregation are not viewed by him as in all respects equal
to their brother prophets. The female is "contained" in
the male, and when separated from it brings chaos and
a threat to the order of things, an order that is controlled by the male. Pagels claims that in those Gnostic
texts where women are urged to "make themselves male"
and the "works of femaleness" are condemned, "the tar-
get is not woman, but the power of sexuality."[77] In saying
that, she misses an important point: Sexuality in most of
these texts is indeed condemned, but it is *female* sexuality
that is rejected, perhaps even by Gnostic and non-Gnostic
Christian ascetic women themselves. Indeed, Thecla, the
heroine of the apocryphal *Acts of Paul and Thecla*, remains a virgin despite attempts on her resolve and her
life, and, conforming to the model of the ascetic male
(i.e., Paul), she "makes herself male," not only in her appearance, by cutting her hair and wearing male clothing,
but in her behavior: In effect, she "flees the works of femaleness."[78] Antoinette Clark Wire claims that the ascetic
"wise women" of texts as diverse as the Hellenistic Jewish *Confession and Prayer of Aseneth* and the Gnostic *Pistis
Sophia*, among others, actually served as a confirmation
of "later [Christian ascetic] women's rejection of sexual-

ity and birth and to legitimate visionary wisdom."[79] In short, like their model and sister Sophia, these representative women attain true wisdom and saving power by "fleeing femaleness," their own powerful sexuality or procreative ability, and "making themselves male." One of the most powerful of the Gnostic female epiphanies of Sophia, the "saved savior" Norea is "the virgin whom the powers did not defile," however she may have appeared in rabbinic Haggadoth.[80] In the *Gospel of Philip,* one of the three Marys who "always walked" with Jesus is his mother, who, like the Holy Spirit, is a virgin (71.15–20; 55.20–35). Like Norea, she is "the virgin whom no power defiled" (55.30). She is also identified with the Holy Spirit and the "double Sophia."[81] The same gospel claims that she is "a great anathema to the Hebrews, who are the apostles and [the] apostolic men," probably the orthodox, who have apparently not understood Mary's "true" role as a purely spiritual being, a "true" virgin. To this paradoxical virgin mother and her role in the economy of salvation we now turn.

Notes

1. When the word *Wisdom* refers to a personification, it will be capitalized; otherwise, it will be lowercased.

2. Burton Mack, *Logos und Sophia: Untersuchungen zur Weisheitstheologie im hellenistischen Judentum*, Studien zur Umwelt des Neuen Testaments, 10 (Göttingen: Vandenhoeck & Ruprecht, 1973), 21. Translations into English are mine.

3. Ibid., 29.

4. See ibid., 29–32.

5. Ibid., 32.

6. Jacob Neusner, *The Incarnation of God: The Character of Divinity in Formative Judaism* (Philadelphia: Fortress Press, 1988), 202.

7. Nehama Aschkenasy, *Eve's Journey: Feminine Images in Hebraic Literary Tradition* (Philadelphia: University of Pennsylvania Press, 1986), 180–82; Judith Hauptmann, "Images of Women in the Talmud," in *Religion and Sexism: Images of Women in the Jewish and Christian Traditions*, ed. Rosemary R. Ruether (New York: Simon & Schuster, 1974), 203–4.

8. Aschkenasy, *Eve's Journey*, 180 n. 22.

9. Ibid., 185.

10. Mack, *Logos und Sophia*, 15, 62–69. See R. E. Witt, *Isis in the Greco-Roman World* (London: Thames & Hudson, 1971), 194–95.

11. John Kloppenborg, "Isis and Sophia in the Book of Wisdom," *HTR* 75 (1982): 81–82.

12. Elisabeth Schüssler Fiorenza, "Wisdom Mythology and the Christological Hymns of the New Testament," in *Aspects of Wisdom in Judaism and Early Christianity*, ed. Robert L. Wilken (Notre Dame, Ind.: University of Notre Dame Press, 1975), 27–30.

13. Richard A. Baer, "Philo's Use of the Categories Male and Female" (Ph.D. diss., Harvard University, 1965), 6. (Published in 1970 under the same title by E. J. Brill, Leiden.)

14. Ibid., 75–100; see Philo, *On Dreams* 1.200; *On Flight and Finding* 51–52, 109; *That the Worse Should be Instructed by the Better* 54; *Allegories of the Laws* 2.49; *Cherubim* 49.

15. Baer, "Philo's Use," 84.

16. Birger A. Pearson, *Philo and the Gnostics on Man and Salvation*, Protocol of the 29th Colloquy of the Center for Hermeneutical Studies in Hellenistic and Modern Culture, 17 April 1977 (Berkeley, Calif.: Graduate Theological Union and University of California Press, 1977), 3–7; Bentley Layton, trans., *The Gnostic Scriptures* (Garden City, N.Y.: Doubleday, 1987), 8.

17. Schüssler Fiorenza, "Wisdom Mythology," 17–41.

18. Carol Meyers, *Discovering Eve: Ancient Israelite Women in Context* (New York: Oxford University Press, 1988), 34.

19. Claudia V. Camp, *Wisdom and the Feminine in the Book of Proverbs*, Bible and Literature Series, 11 (Sheffield: JSOT/Almond Press, 1985), 75.

20. Meyers, *Discovering Eve;* Aschkenasy, *Eve's Journey;* Camp, *Wisdom;* Elisabeth Schüssler Fiorenza, *In Memory of Her: A Feminist Theological Reconstruction of Christian Origins* (New York: Crossroad, 1983).

21. Meyers, *Discovering Eve,* 149–50.

22. Ibid., 91.

23. Aschkenasy, *Eve's Journey,* 13. Although Aschkenasy does not suggest this possibility, the victory song of Miriam in Ex. 15:20–21, perhaps the oldest piece of Israelite poetry in the Tanak, may also reflect this tradition.

24. See Claudia V. Camp, "Female Sage and Biblical Wisdom" (Paper presented at the Male and Female in Gnosticism Section, AAR/SBL Annual Meeting, Chicago, Ill., Nov. 17–20, 1988).

25. Camp, *Wisdom,* 81.

26. Aschkenasy, *Eve's Journey,* 176–77.

27. Ibid., 174.

28. Ibid., 166; Camp, *Wisdom,* 126.

29. Aschkenasy, *Eve's Journey,* 156.

30. Camp, *Wisdom,* 99–103.

31. See ibid., 119.

32. Ibid., 105–9.

33. Ibid., 240–41; Meyers, *Discovering Eve*, 180–87.

34. See Helmut Koester, "The Structure and Criteria of Early Christian Beliefs," in James M. Robinson and Helmut Koester, *Trajectories Through Early Christianity* (Philadelphia: Fortress Press, 1971), 221.

35. Schüssler Fiorenza, *In Memory of Her*, 134–35.

36. Burton Mack, "Q and Christian Origins," in *Early Christianity, Jesus, and Q*, Semeia, 54 (Atlanta: Scholars Press, forthcoming).

37. Hal Taussig, "Sophia and Her Children in Q" (Paper presented at the Male and Female in Gnosticism Section, AAR/SBL Annual Meeting, Chicago, Ill., Nov. 17–20, 1988).

38. Mack, "Q and Christian Origins," 5–7.

39. Trans. Koester, "Structure and Criteria," 221; slightly modified.

40. Ibid., 222.

41. Ibid.

42. James M. Robinson, "Very Goddess and Very Man: Jesus' Better Self," in *Images of the Feminine in Gnosticism*, ed. Karen L. King, Studies in Antiquity and Christianity (Philadelphia: Fortress Press, 1988), 119.

43. For a more complete and detailed comparison of the Jewish and Gnostic Sophias, see George W. MacRae, "The Jewish Background of the Sophia Myth," *Novum Testamentum* 12 (1970): 86–101.

44. Richard Smith, "Sex Education in Gnostic Schools," in King, ed., *Images*, 358–60.

45. Trans. Hans-Gebhard Bethge and Orval S. Wintermute, in *The Nag Hammadi Library in English*, ed. James M. Robinson (San Francisco: Harper & Row, 1977), 161–79. (Hereafter abbreviated *NHL*.)

46. Michael A. Williams, "Variety in Gnostic Perspectives on Gender," in King, ed., *Images*, 21–22.

47. Deirdre A. Good, *Reconstructing the Traditions of Sophia*, SBLMS, 32 (Atlanta, Ga.: Scholars Press, 1987), 76.

48. Trans. Richard L. Arthur, in *Nag Hammadi Corpus*, 6.2, in Rose Horman Arthur, *The Wisdom Goddess* (Lanham, Md.: University Press of America, 1984), 218.

49. Jorunn Jacobsen Buckley, "The Holy Spirit Is a Double Name," in King, ed., *Images*, 211–12, 221–22.

50. Good, *Reconstructing,* 76–78.

51. See Wayne Meeks, "The Image of the Androgyne," *HR* 13 (1974): 206–8; Buckley, "Holy Spirit," 212.

52. Aydeet Fischer-Mueller, "The Gnostic Sophia: Suffering Sister of Hokhmah and Eve" (Paper presented at the Male and Female in Gnosticism Section, AAR/SBL Annual Meeting, Chicago, Ill., Nov. 17–20, 1988).

53. Ibid.

54. Good, *Reconstructing,* 67. Valentinus (ca. 100–175 C.E.) was an influential Gnostic Christian teacher and preacher from Alexandria who later went to Rome. He and his followers accepted Christian traditions and scripture, but sought their "higher" meaning through a system of allegorical interpretation. For a more complete description of Valentinus, his works, his philosophy, and his "school," see Layton, trans., *Gnostic Scriptures,* 217–22, 267–75.

55. Trans. John D. Turner, *NHL,* 188–94.

56. Trans. Roger A. Bullard, *NHL,* 329–38.

57. Trans. Layton, *Gnostic Scriptures,* 28–51. Material in square brackets indicates my insertions.

58. Ibid., 68–76.

59. Anne McGuire, "Virginity and Subversion: Norea Against the Powers in the *Hypostasis of the Archons,*" in King, ed., *Images,* 257.

60. Trans. Bethge and Wintermute, *NHL,* 161–79.

61. Birger A. Pearson, "Revisiting Norea," in King, ed., *Images,* 268; see Good, *Reconstructing,* 76–78.

62. Trans. Harold W. Attridge and Dieter Mueller, *NHL,* 54–97.

63. Trans. George W. MacRae, *NHL,* 37–49.

64. Trans. Attridge, *NHL,* 229–38.

65. Trans. William R. Schoedel, *NHL,* 242–48.

66. Trans. Malcolm L. Peel and Jan Zandee, *NHL,* 346–61.

67. Trans. John D. Turner, *NHL,* 435–40.

68. Trans. Wesley W. Isenberg, *NHL,* 131–51.

69. Ibid.

70. Elaine H. Pagels, *The Gnostic Gospels* (New York: Random House, 1979), 64.

71. Trans. Attridge, *NHL,* 229–38.

72. Trans. George W. MacRae and R. McL. Wilson, *NHL,* 471–74.

73. Trans. Thomas O. Lambdin, *NHL*, 117–30.

74. Pagels, *Gnostic Gospels*, 64.

75. Montanus (ca. 172 C.E.), together with the prophetesses Prisca and Maximilla, is associated with the New Prophecy movement (Montanism) arising in Phrygia (Asia Minor) toward the end of the second century. Laying claim to the tradition of prophecy through the Holy Spirit in Christianity, they announced the imminent return of Christ, and attempted to imitate the prophetic, apocalyptic, and ascetic life-style of the earliest Christians. Montanism was regarded as a heresy by the orthodox Christians.

76. See Buckley, "Holy Spirit," 216–18.

77. Pagels, *Gnostic Gospels*, 66–67.

78. See Meeks, "Image of the Androgyne," 196.

79. Antoinette Clark Wire, "The Social Functions of Women's Asceticism in the Roman East," in King, ed., *Images*, 308–23.

80. Pearson, "Revisiting Norea," 266.

81. Buckley, "Holy Spirit," 211.

4

"Mother and Maiden Was Never None But She": The Many Marys

Woman, what have you to do with me?
—John 2:4a

The Mary of History and Faith: The New Testament Witness

The Gospels of the New Testament, together with the writings of Paul, center upon Jesus as the Christ and the meanings of that person and that title for the Christian communities represented by the canon. Canonization of texts inevitably involves selectivity, but a selection process went into the texts long before they became canon, even before they became written. It is by now a truism of biblical scholarship that the Jesus of history is barely tangential to the Christ of faith: that the writings that eventually became the New Testament reflect many levels, needs, and concerns of the communities that grew out of the movement Jesus began. Nevertheless, for the New Testament, Jesus is the fulcrum of the history of salvation, both in his resurrection, the primary datum of the Christian faith, and in his incarnation. It should be remembered, however, that the New Testament witnesses, central though they may have become, especially in the Protestant churches, are not the only or even the best witnesses to the many varieties of Christianity in its formative period. Moreover, while the books of the New Testament, or at any rate the earlier writings, do not consciously formulate doctrine, they do reflect the doctrinal interests of the orthodoxy that was shaping itself in the second to the fourth centuries of the common era. Hence, the New Testament as canon is largely a second- to fourth-century product, although the traditions embodied in it are older.

Such considerations have naturally played a role in biblical scholarship, especially that scholarship, once again largely Protestant, that has concerned itself in this century with the quest of the "historical Jesus." Protestant scholars and theologians have been less enthusiastic about the quest for other "historical" figures, particularly Mary, Jesus' mother, who has largely been a preoccupation with Roman Catholic scholarship. As Michael P. Carroll has observed of this difference,

> Protestant theologians have always had two strong objections to the Mary cult. The first is that there is little or no basis for such a cult in the New Testament.... The second is historical: there is little or no evidence that anything like the Mary cult existed during the first four centuries of the Christian Church.[1]

Carroll is actually overstating his case, especially in his second objection, since he is concerned only with the emergence of a full-blown *cultus* of the Virgin Mary, which he finds in the fifth century, beginning with her recognition as *Theotokos* (God-bearer) by the Council of Chalcedon (451). Nevertheless, he is correct in seeing that there is little mention of Mary in the New Testament, and most of what is said about her in orthodox patristic and even in heterodox sources, at least until the latter part of the second century, is "chiefly in connection with christological questions."[2] Indeed, the major source that expresses an interest in Mary's life prior to the birth of Jesus, which nevertheless is its climax, is the second-century apocryphal "pregospel," the *Protevangelium of James*. Representations of Mary in early Christian art are scarce until the fifth century because of a preoccupation with resurrection rather than incarnation. When such representations do appear, they nevertheless seem to support purely christological themes such as the incarnation, since Mary never appears in art without Jesus until after the first half of the fifth century.[3]

Before we can suggest, even tentatively, why Mary plays a much larger role in noncanonical literature and theology than she does in the New Testament itself, we necessarily have to see what kind of role she actually does play in the canonical writings. Let us begin with the earliest witness who refers to Jesus' mother, Paul. In examining his references, which are mainly indirect and never mention Mary by name, we need to remember that Paul was not very much interested in the earthly Jesus, "Christ according to the flesh" (2 Cor. 2:16), either. Although Paul refers to "James, the Lord's brother" (Gal. 1:19), he directly refers to Jesus' mother only once; the reference also occurs in Galatians (4:4–5), in the context of his polemic against the Law: "But when the fullness of time had come, God sent his Son, born of a woman, born under the law, in order to redeem [purchase] those who were under the law, so that we might receive adoption as children" (NRSV; Greek has "sonship"). By his reference to adoption by God through the "Spirit of the son," Paul effectively nullifies any importance that might be attached to biological birth from a woman. His other reference to birth "according to the flesh" also occurs in Galatians, in his allegory of Sarah and Hagar, Sarah representing the birth of the son "according to the spirit," and Hagar, the slave-wife of Abraham, representing the birth of the son "according to the flesh" (4:28–31). Fleshly, human birth definitely belongs to a lower order for Paul. The only other reference Paul makes to Jesus' birth "according to the flesh" is in Romans 1:3–4, in the context of what appears to be a confessional statement: Christ is "born from David's seed according to the flesh and declared to be Son of God in power according to the spirit of holiness by resurrection from the dead." Clearly, for Paul, the spiritual birth is of greater importance.

In the Gospel of Mark, the earliest of the written canonical Gospels, Mary's role is minimal, and she belongs to that group close to Jesus that persistently misunderstands his true nature, both as Son of God in the present and as Son of man, the lord of the future. In Mark 3:20–30, after appointing the Twelve, Jesus has "gone home" to Nazareth. There, a large crowd comes together, "so that they could not even eat." Jesus' family, when they hear of this, "went out to restrain him, for people were saying, 'He has gone out of his mind.'" Jesus' family's misperception is linked in this passage to the misunderstanding of the "scribes from Jerusalem," who charge, "He has Beelzebul, and by the ruler of the demons he casts out demons." The latter misunderstanding, and by implication that of his family, stands under Jesus' pronouncement of judgment for blasphemy against the Holy Spirit, "for they had said, 'He has an unclean spirit'" (3:30, NRSV). In the pericope that follows (3:31–35), Jesus' biological family again appears: "Then his mother and his brothers came; and standing outside, they sent to him and called him." It is not clear whether they have just now arrived, having gone out to "restrain" him, but it is clear that Jesus will have none of them. He prefers instead the "eschatological family" of those who will understand and follow his radical rejection of biological and social ties in favor of pursuing the kingdom of God:[4]

> A crowd was sitting around him; and they said to him, "Your mother and your brothers and your sisters are outside, asking for you." And he replied, "Who are my mother and my brothers?" And looking at those who sat around him, he said, "Here are my mother and my brothers! Whoever does the will of God is my brother and sister and mother." (Mark 3:32–35, NRSV; see Mark 10:29–30)

Just as Jesus is misunderstood by his biological family in Mark, so also he is misunderstood and rejected by the people of his hometown, who are "amazed" at his "wisdom" and "deeds of power," questioning their source, as well as Jesus' own origin: " 'Is not this the carpenter, the son of Mary and brother of James and Joses and Judas and Simon, and are not his sisters here with us?' and they took offense at him" (6:2–3, NRSV). This rejection in Mark acts as the context of Jesus' saying about the prophet without honor: "Prophets are not without honor, except in their hometown, and among their own kin, and in their own house" (6:4, NRSV). He is in turn "astonished" by their unbelief, which renders him unable to perform any exorcisms (6:5–6a). This episode of rejection at Nazareth, besides giving us the most complete list of Jesus' siblings, may also echo a tradition that comes out for the most part in Jewish extracanonical and polemical sources from a later period. We refer to the tradition of Jesus' illegitimacy, the *Toledoth Yeshu*. The designation "son of Mary," which is modified to "son of Joseph" in Luke (4:22) and "carpenter's son" in Matthew (13:55), seems to point vaguely to such a tradition, which is not pursued, even in an apologetic way, by Mark, as it is by Matthew and Luke, both of whom emphasize Mary's

virginal conception of Jesus.[5] In any event, this may be
the last appearance of Jesus' mother in the Gospel of
Mark, unless the Mary who is designated "the mother of
James the younger and Joses," witness to the crucifixion,
burial, and empty tomb (Mark 15:40, 47; 16:1), is also
the mother of Jesus. Of these references, the first would
seem definitely to rule out Jesus' mother, who is certainly
mother of a James, but presumably the one who is always
designated "the elder." In Mark 15:47, however, she is
referred to only as "the mother of Joses," and in 16:1,
again as "the mother of James." The other Synoptists do
not provide us with much help: In the Matthean parallel, Matthew 27:56, she is "mother of James and Joseph,"
while in the Lukan parallel, Luke 24:10, one of the three
named women at the empty tomb is "Mary the mother of
James." Only in John 19:25 is she unambiguously identified as "Jesus' mother."[6] Whether Mark was referring to
Jesus' mother by these roundabout references cannot be
determined with any certainty. In fact, the very vague-
ness of the references may be intended to distance Jesus,
as Son of God, from his earthly parentage.

If the references to Mary in Mark's Gospel are sketchy
at best and appear negative, those in Matthew and Luke,
especially the latter, give Mary a larger role, but one that
emphasizes her virginal conception of Jesus and her relationship to him as a disciple, both at the expense of
depicting her reality as his mother. Matthew's narrative,
consistent with the theology of his Gospel, sets the birth
of Jesus in the context of the salvation history of Israel.
His genealogy in 1:1–17 is unusual in that it includes, in
its list of fathers, four mothers: Tamar, by whom, using
Matthew's language, Judah was the father of Perez and
Zerah (1:3); Rahab, by whom Salmon was the father of
Boaz (1:5); Ruth, by whom Boaz fathered Obed; and "the
wife of Uriah," as Matthew refers to Bathsheba, by whom
David fathered Solomon (1:6). The list leads up to the
birth of Jesus (1:16) with an interesting circumlocution:
"Jacob [was] the father of Joseph the husband of Mary, of

whom Jesus was born, who is called the messiah [Christ]." Clearly Matthew is cancelling out Joseph as the biological father of Jesus, but not Mary as the biological mother. The roles played in the salvation history of Israel by the four mothers who precede Mary are also highlighted by Matthew, in his characteristic linking of Jesus to Israelite history and prophecy as their culmination. But why these particular four?

All four share, with Mary, a certain "irregularity" with respect to their social roles. Tamar posed as a prostitute in order to seduce Judah, her father-in-law, who had refused to honor his obligation to provide her with his third son, Shelah, as her husband. In the story as told in Genesis 38, Tamar's "irregular" action eventually secures her right, and her righteousness is confirmed by Judah, who declares that "she is more righteous than I" (Gen. 38:26). The twins Tamar bears secure the "redemption" of her line. Philo of Alexandria, somewhat paradoxically, considers her as a model of the "undefiled and truly virginal" (*De Cong.* 124), much as he considers Wisdom herself.[7] The only Rahab who is mentioned in the Tanak is "Rahab the harlot," the prostitute of Jericho in Joshua 2:1–14, who saves the life of the Israelite spies because of her faith in YHWH, the God of Israel. For her action, she also is instrumental in "delivering from death" the lives of her entire family (Josh. 6:25). Rahab thus is another example of a woman who employs irregular means to preserve the safety of her household. Ruth most certainly, as previously noted, is the "cause of redemption" of her line and that of Naomi, through her seduction of Boaz. As the women of Bethlehem congratulate Naomi on the birth of her "redeemer," Obed, from the "one who is more to you than seven sons" (Ruth 4:14–15, NRSV), so also the elders pray that Ruth may, like Rachel and Leah, "build up the house of Israel," and that Boaz and Ruth's house "be like the house of Perez, whom Tamar bore to Judah" (4:11–12). Once again, as the reference to Tamar indicates, salvation and continuance of life, the province of the "mother in Israel," are achieved by somewhat sexually "irregular" means, outside of traditional marriage. The final example, that of Bathsheba, whom Matthew merely calls "wife of Uriah," certainly points to sexual irregularity, but it is irregular behavior on the part of King David, rather than any action on the part of Bathsheba herself. As the story is told in 2 Samuel 11:2–12:25, Bathsheba is merely the object of lust of the king, whose actions are the raw exercise of royal power: David desires her; he sends for her; he "[lies] with her"; and, when she becomes pregnant, he contrives to have her husband, Uriah—who will not lie with his wife in order to legitimate the child she carries—killed. Furthermore, when David does marry Bathsheba, the child that is thus "legitimated" dies, as punishment for David, who deserves to die, but repents (12:14). Solomon, the second child of Bathsheba and David, is born after David "consoled his wife Bathsheba, and went to her, and lay with her" (12:24, NRSV).[8]

The story of the "husband of Mary" and her son forms the first part of Matthew's birth narrative, in which the focus is more on Joseph than on Mary, is on his suspicion of her adultery, the angelic message confirming her virginity, and their resulting lack of sexual relations before Jesus' birth (Matt. 1:18–25). But why would Matthew want to introduce this story by prefacing it with those of the four mothers of Israel, especially the last one, Bathsheba, who is characterized more as a wife (of Uriah) than a mother? Perhaps Matthew, like the *Midrash ha-Gadol* (1.334–39), had a list of "women of valor" that included these women, and he expanded it to include Mary.[9] Yet this explanation will not cover Matthew's emphasis on husbands (or nonhusbands) and fathers (or a nonfather, as in the case of Joseph). The writers of *Mary in the New Testament* believe that the women of Matthew 1:1–17 are those who, "marked by irregular marital unions, were vehicles of God's messianic plan."[10] This explanation, while more satisfactory in its emphasis on the irregular, on the women whose conception "breaks the pattern," nevertheless, as Jane Schaberg points out, does not quite fit Matthew's narrative, since he is not emphasizing *marital* union, especially in the case of Joseph and Mary, where he appears rather to emphasize their *lack* of union.[11] As far as these women being "vehicles of God's messianic plan," the metaphor of "vehicle" would certainly fit the passivity of Bathsheba and Matthew's Mary, but not the activity of Tamar, Rahab, and Ruth. Schaberg suggests that Matthew may have in mind a situation for these women that poses a danger to men: They represent a sexuality that is not yet "properly related"—that is, under the control of a male. These women (and their offspring) needed to be "sanctified" by proper direction and relation to a male, within the male-dominant order of their respective societies.[12] In Mary's case, it is God himself who sanctifies, through the Holy Spirit that works through others in the history of Israel, the apparently "irregularly" born child. Like the women of the genealogy, Mary will, through her motherhood, be instrumental in the salvation of Israel: Her child especially "will save his people from their sins," being named Jesus (Yeshua), for "he saves" (Matt. 18:21).

We need not here discuss the possibility that Matthew, like Luke, may have been responding to allegations or traditions of Jesus' illegitimacy.[13] Even without considering that possibility we can see that Matthew intended the birth of the savior to be one that is paradoxically consistent with other events in the salvation history of Israel: God, for Matthew, frames human actions in a paradoxical way. Just as Jesus, the messiah of Israel, was conceived paradoxically, so his rejection as messiah by Israel is a paradoxical means of the salvation of "all the nations" (Gentiles). Just as no one in Israel expected a messiah to be crucified (although they may have expected him to be martyred), so no one expected a virginal mother for the messiah: Matthew's interpretation of Isaiah 7:14 in Matthew 1:23 thus reflects what Fredriksen has called

his "peculiar messianic teleology."[14] Matthew begins with
the given that Jesus is the messiah. He also knows the tradition that a woman named Mary is his mother, and that
there is something "irregular" connected with that birth.
The authors of *Mary in the New Testament* suggest that,
even prior to the composition of the Gospel, there was a
tradition of the virginal conception of Jesus, which Matthew uniquely made part of his portrayal of the messianic
nature of Jesus, a portrayal supported throughout his
Gospel by constant references to prophecy.[15] He understands *parthenos*, the Greek translation of the Hebrew
'almah ("Behold, the virgin will conceive and will give
birth to a son, and will call his name Emmanuel" [Isa.
7:14], English trans. of the Masoretic text), as "virgin"
in conception, as his emphasis on Joseph's *not* being the
father indicates.[16]

Matthew's interest in Mary's role in the paradoxical
furthering of Israel's (and the Gentiles') salvation carries
only through the birth narratives. In the visit of the Magi
(Matt. 2:1–12), the "wise men from the East" are searching for the child, whom they find "with Mary his mother,"
but they kneel to do homage to the child, as "king of the
Jews," not his mother (2:11). In the earliest of Christian
art depicting Mary and Jesus, the favored theme seems
to have been this one—"the manifestation of the Christ to
the Gentiles"—in which Mary serves (as in the Matthean
text) as background, vehicle, or instrument to show her
child, the infant king.[17] The focus in these paintings, as
in Matthew's narrative, is upon the interaction between
the child and the world, not upon Mary.

In Matthew's narrative it is Joseph who is warned,
again by an angelic message, to "take the child and his
mother" to Egypt, to escape Herod's impending mas-
sacre of the infants in his angry desire to eliminate possible rivals for kingship of the Jews (Matt. 2:13–15). Once
again, Mary (this time referred to merely as Jesus' mother
and not by name) appears in the narrative only in asso-
ciation with "the child" and not in an active role. The

language and pattern are repeated in 2:19–23, where Joseph, once more warned in a dream, is advised to bring "the child and his mother" back to the land of Israel and finally to Nazareth in Galilee.

After this end to the birth narrative, Mary virtually disappears from Matthew, except for brief appearances (unnamed) in the episode on Jesus' true family, a parallel to Mark 3:31–35 and Luke 8:19–21, and in that of Jesus' rejection at Nazareth, the setting for the saying on the prophet without honor in 13:54–58 (parallels in Mark 6:1–6a; Luke 4:16–30). As previously noted, Matthew downplays the hint of illegitimacy offered in the rejection story in Mark. He does this by changing the skeptical questions of the people: "Is this not the carpenter's son? Is not his mother called Mary? And are not his brothers James and Joseph and Simon and Judas? And are not all his sisters with us? Where then did this man get all this [wisdom and deeds of power]?" (NRSV). For Matthew, as for Mark, these questions reveal the misunderstanding of Jesus as messiah, even by the people of his hometown, but of particular interest for Matthew is the question of Jesus' birth: The reader "knows" that Jesus is *not* the "carpenter's son"; his mother, however, truly is Mary, but her role as mother is not emphasized. It is further unclear whether Mary is among the women "looking on at a distance" at Jesus' crucifixion in Matthew 27:55–56, women who "had followed Jesus from Galilee and had provided for him," or whether she is "the other Mary" mentioned with Mary Magdalene at the tomb in 27:61 and 28:1. This "other" Mary may be the same one as the Mary in 27:56, who is mentioned as "Mary the mother of James and Joseph," a phrase that might be a circumlocution for Jesus' mother since he has brothers named "James and Joseph" in 13:55. However, if this odd designation is meant to indicate that Mary is Jesus' mother as well, its very circumlocutory nature serves subtly to further dissociate him from her: This dissociation is reinforced by the acclaim of Jesus as "God's Son" by

the centurion in 27:54. If Jesus is the Son of God, he is at
this point in the narrative no longer designated the son
of Mary.

Although Matthew accords Mary some role in his salvation history, if only as the mother of the messiah, whose
conception and birth came about somewhat irregularly
in the eyes of the world, it is Luke who emphasizes in
his birth narrative not only the role of Mary, but also
her virginity, to a degree much greater than Matthew
does. In the parallel stories of the conception and birth of
John the Baptist and Jesus, Luke, like Matthew, emphasizes "irregularity," but not marital or sexual irregularity.
By placing the announcement of the apparently barren
Elizabeth's impending conception of John by Zechariah
first, Luke focuses upon the extraordinary nature of this
event, paralleled in other extraordinary conceptions by
barren women, beginning with Isaac (Gen. 18:1–15), and
continuing with Samson (Judg. 13) and Samuel (1 Sam.
1:1–2:11). John is linked especially with Samson and
Samuel through the repetition of the "Nazirite vow" in
his proposed dedication to the service of the Lord (Luke
1:15). Although Mary is not barren, but a betrothed
virgin, her conception of Jesus is linked to Elizabeth's
conception of John, both by Gabriel's announcement
of Elizabeth's pregnancy and Mary's impending one,
which tells Mary that "nothing will be impossible with
God," and by Mary's Song (Luke 2:46–55) following
the visit of Elizabeth, which recalls the song of the for-
merly barren Hannah in 1 Samuel 2:1–10, a song that
might belong more properly in the mouth of the barren Elizabeth. With this parallelism, Luke appears to
suggest that extraordinary modes of birth are indeed
the province of God through the Holy Spirit, which for
him guides and directs all of salvation history. The announcements of the angels to Zechariah and to Mary
recall announcements "to the mothers of the great figures of the OT; . . . [these proclaim] the forthcoming birth
of a child who would have a unique place in salva-

tion history."[18] In addition, Elizabeth's greeting to Mary ("Blessed are you among women"), which gives Mary (and her child) special prominence in that salvation history, recalls similar pronouncements to "women famous in Israelite history who have helped to deliver God's people from peril," including Jael ("Most blessed of women be Jael" [Judg. 5:24]) and Judith ("O daughter, you are blessed by the Most High God above all other women on earth" [Judith 13:18, NRSV]).[19] This greeting is echoed by Mary's words, "Surely from now on all generations will call me blessed" (1:48), and by the greeting of Gabriel, "Rejoice, favored one! The Lord is with you!" (1:28), which is followed in some Greek manuscripts and in the Latin version by Jerome (the Vulgate) by the words, "Blessed are you among women." The "deliverer" of a child is thus linked to the women who have had roles in "delivering" their people: Mary takes her place with them as a "mother in Israel."

Yet Mary's role as "mother in Israel" is one that is, like those of other "mothers," especially the barren ones, linked to the action of God, who chooses the lowly in preference to the proud. The celebration of God's saving activity in Israel by Mary's son (1:46–55), particularly in its connection with the Song of Hannah in 1 Samuel 2:1–10, focuses upon the choice and elevation of the *tapeinous* (lowly). God has looked upon the *tapeinosis* (lowliness) of Mary, God's servant (1:48), as upon all in a similar state. I agree here with Schaberg that the reference to Mary's low and even humiliated estate, together with the links to Elizabeth and to other "humiliated" women whom God restored through granting or preserving the life of a child—Hannah (the "servant of the Lord" [1 Sam. 1:11]), Leah (Gen. 29:32), and Hagar (Gen. 16:11)—is meant by Luke to fit into his general theological theme: the positive bent of God toward the humiliated and oppressed.[20] It has been suggested that Mary's Song, which probably preexisted Luke's Gospel, represents the piety of the *Anawim* (the poor ones), those at the bottom of society who yet regarded themselves as utterly dependent upon and faithful to YHWH. This piety is exhibited in similar hymnic compositions from Qumran, including the *Hodayoth,* the Thanksgiving Psalms, whose author identifies himself as one of the *'ebyonim* or *Anawim* (1 QH 2:34–35).[21] Among Jewish Christians, these "poor ones," known as Ebionites, developed a severely ascetic life-style suited to their paucity of resources; this life-style elevated poverty as sanctity and proof of election.[22]

Certainly the first epiphany of Jesus in the Gospel of Luke can be seen as expressing this theology, although the narrative in Luke 2:1–20 can stand on its own as a birth story, and judging from the differences and repetitions that link it to chapter 1, it may originally have done so.[23] In this narrative, Joseph and the pregnant Mary are forced to return to Bethlehem because of a census for tax purposes. Although this census is anachronistic (a census of Judea occurred in 6 C.E.), it is probably meant to be symbolic: Unlike the actual census under Quirinius, it is global in scope, including "all the world," as does the Roman power. Luke must also have remembered the revolt caused by the real census in 6. Perhaps the setting of the birth, in a stable at Bethlehem, an appropriate milieu for the "poor ones," is subtly in contrast to the might and power of Roman oppression.[24] The shepherds—those to whom the angelic chorus announces the "sign" of the presence of the savior, the messiah, the Lord who is present in humble circumstances, albeit in the birthplace of King David—are themselves virtual outcasts. The shepherds serve two functions in the narrative: They remind the reader that David was himself a shepherd at Bethlehem when God designated him king; they also belong to a group of people regarded by the interpreters of the Law as outside of it, incapable of bearing witness in court because of their alleged dishonesty.[25] It may be for this reason that Luke is so anxious to demonstrate the fidelity of Jesus' family to the Law: the circumcision of the eight-day-old male (2:21); the purification sacrifice and redemption of the firstborn son, as commanded in Exodus 13:1, 11–16, and Leviticus 12:2–8 (2:22–24); and the celebration of the pilgrim festival of the Passover in Jerusalem (2:41–51). As Gerd Theissen has remarked, the confrontation between the alien culture of Rome and Jewish society in first-century Judea led to an "intensifying [of] those norms which are characteristic for Jewish society," but incapable of being realized by most of it. This divided Jewish society in Israel into two groups: the *am-ha-'aretz* (the "people of the land who do not know the Law") and those who kept the Law.[26] Luke therefore wishes to demonstrate that Jesus' family may belong to those in socially reduced circumstances, but they are *Anawim,* not *am-ha-'aretz:* They keep the Law.

One aspect of the presentation in the Temple episode (2:22–24) deserves special note, as it concerns Luke's own traditions and later traditions about Mary. Luke appears to conflate the sacrifice for purification required after a woman has a male child (Lev. 12:2–8; see Luke 2:22, 24) and the "redemption of the firstborn," the price of five shekels paid to "buy back" from YHWH the firstborn male (Num. 18:15–16; see Luke 2:23). Either, as may be likely, Luke was anxious to show Mary and Joseph as pious *Anawim* but was confused as to exactly what sacrifices they were being pious about, and in any case did not care, or he was not dwelling so much upon the need for Mary's purification, since her child was not conceived in an ordinary manner. That does not indicate that Luke was necessarily thinking of Mary's virginity *in partu* (during the birth of Jesus), as later church tradition interpreted him to mean.[27] All that it probably means is that, for Luke, the focus of his narrative is upon the setting, the Temple, and the revelation of the savior of Israel in the heart of Israel.

It is this revelation sequence, the prophecy of Simeon (2:25–35) and that of Anna (2:36–38), that provides a context for a secondary revelation, one to Mary. Simeon specifically turns to Mary, having praised God for the birth of the "salvation" of Israel in terms that "amaze" Jesus' family, and says to her: "This child is destined for the falling and the rising of many in Israel, and to be a sign that will be opposed so that the inner thoughts of many will be revealed—and a sword will pierce your own soul too" (2:34–35, NRSV). Mary's role in this scene forms a parallel to two other scenes of revelation and astonishment: the revelation of the shepherds (2:16–19) and the finding of Jesus in the Temple (2:41–51). In all three, Mary appears first as an astonished and then as a thoughtful witness to events that show her son to be the savior. In the first, the shepherds, obedient to the heavenly message, come to Bethlehem to see the child. "When they saw this, they made known what had been told them about this child; and all who heard it were amazed at what the shepherds told them" (2:17–18, NRSV). Mary's response, however, is different: "But Mary kept all these words, pondering them in her heart" (2:19). It is not said how Mary reacted to Simeon's message to her; nor is it entirely clear what the "sword" is that will pierce her own soul, only that it will happen as a result of her son, the "sign" that reveals "the inner thoughts of many" (2:35). Perhaps Luke intends this reference to look forward to the divisions that will occur before the destruction of the Temple (21:12–24), but it is impossible to say how it refers to Mary specifically, unless to her inclusion or exclusion from Jesus' "eschatological family," which depends on hearing and doing the will of God (8:19–21; 11:27–28).[28] Since Mary has been obedient to the will of God from the beginning (e.g., 1:38), it is difficult to conclude that her obedience or fidelity as a disciple was being tested: After all, in her case maternal loyalty to her son, filial piety toward God, and discipleship coincide.

In the last of the three episodes, that in which Jesus is found in the Temple (2:41–51), Jesus is revealed as the one who is divinely instructed in wisdom and is himself the instructor of wisdom. When his parents find him, he has "amazed" the teachers "by his understanding and his answers." Mary here plays an active role. Getting over her initial astonishment, she questions him: "Child, why have you treated us like this? Look, your father and I have been searching for you in great anxiety" (2:48). In the context of Luke's narrative, these words are fraught with meaning: They give Jesus the opportunity to reveal that he is in his true Father's house, and they explicitly include Mary as one who "did not understand what he said to them" (2:49). By enclosing this episode with direct references to Jesus' increase in wisdom (2:40; 2:52), Luke also rejects Mary, along with anyone else, as Jesus' potential instructor in wisdom. Finally, as the episode closes, Mary once again "kept all these things in her heart" (2:51).

In these three episodes Mary is specifically referred to as the recipient of some special revelation about her son that she does not quite understand. What do these episodes mean? Both Schaberg and the authors of *Mary in the New Testament* believe that Luke is presenting Mary as a "disciple, the believer, esteemed for hearing the word of God and doing it" (11:27–28). She may not at first perceive the meaning of Jesus, but—through fidelity to God's revelation and obedience to God's will—she grows in understanding and God's favor, as does her son.[29] It is difficult to see this as a positive portrait, especially in the light of Jesus' rejection of his biological family in 8:19–21, and his biological mother specifically in 11:27–28. In the latter passage, which follows the Beelzebul controversy (11:14–26), a "woman in the crowd" utters words that recall Elizabeth's words to Mary: "Blessed is the womb that bore you, and the breasts that nursed you!" (11:27, NRSV). Jesus' reply clearly distances him from his mother and any blessing connected with her: "Blessed rather are those who hear the word of God and obey it!" (11:28, NRSV).

Luke places Mary quite definitely among the ranks of the "blessed among women" in God's plan of salvation. Why, then, does he appear equally definitely to reject her? One answer may be derived from the interaction of

Luke's generally favorable attitude toward women and the preservation, from the Q tradition, of a certain radical rejection of family and motherhood as traditionally understood. As Elisabeth Schüssler Fiorenza has pointed out, "Faithful discipleship, not biological motherhood, is the eschatological calling of women" for Luke.[30] Can then Mary, Jesus' biological mother, be considered a faithful disciple? Is that the portrait of Mary with which Luke wants to leave the reader? Certainly Mary's obedience to the word and will of God is emphasized in the infancy narratives, especially in 1:38, where she calls herself a "(female) slave" (*doule*) of God; this submissive utterance struck a particularly favorable chord in later patristic exegesis, which loved to compare the "obedient" (and passive) Mary to the "disobedient" (and active) Eve (e.g., Justin, *Dialogue with Trypho* 100.5; Irenaeus, *Against Heresies* 3.21.10; 3.22.4). Women's discipleship in Luke seems to be mainly of the passive, receptive variety, as exemplified in the story of Martha and Mary in 10:38–42, with the latter sitting at Jesus' feet and hearing his words. In just such a way Mary, Jesus' mother, seems to passively receive words, as she "received" the "power of the Most High" to conceive Jesus. She "keeps" the words in her heart, and "ponders" or "revolves" them (*symballousa*). We are never told by Luke what conclusions, if any, Mary reaches about these words, or how she acts on them. Although she does appear with the disciples in Acts 1:14, it is not clear that she is even included in the group of women who "follow" Jesus from Galilee (Luke 8:1–3), who stand "at a distance, watching these things," at the crucifixion (23:49), who see the tomb and the burial (23:55), and who are witnesses to the empty tomb (24:10). As noted above, it is indeed unclear whether "Mary the mother of James" referred to in 24:10 is in fact also the mother of Jesus. In any case, this designation would distance her further from Jesus.

It would appear, then, that Luke throughout the Gospel increases Jesus' distance from Mary, beginning with the episode of finding Jesus in the Temple. Once

Jesus rebukes his mother for not knowing that he would be in his Father's house, a remark that Mary inexplicably does not understand (after all, she had been clearly told by Gabriel that the child so miraculously conceived would be called "Son of the Most High" [1:32]), she decreases as he "increases in wisdom and in stature" (2:52). What is the point of Luke's emphasis on Mary's keeping things in her heart and "putting them together" (*symballousa* [2:19]), only to drop her, even as a passive participant, in the rest of the Gospel? Schaberg, who also sees how uneasily the first two chapters of Luke sit with the rest of his Gospel, claims that they, with their emphasis on Mary, were meant to "defend Mary's honor" against the charge of unchastity and hence Jesus against charges of illegitimacy.[31] If that is the case, there is really little necessity for the second chapter, which focuses on the revelation of Jesus as the savior of all of Israel, particularly the *Anawim,* and of the Gentiles. I would suggest rather that Luke has inherited two birth stories, or perhaps has inherited one birth story (the narrative in 2:1–20), and has put together another (the narrative in chap. 1) by weaving together inherited traditions about John the Baptist and Jesus, which may have included a preexisting hymn, the Song of Mary (1:46–55), attributed to Elizabeth in some manuscripts.[32] In the narratives of chapter 1, the emphasis appears to be upon Elizabeth and Mary as "mothers in Israel," sources of salvation. Although Elizabeth's role appears to be secondary to that of Zechariah in the narrative as it now stands, he nevertheless is presented as the one who doubts the angel's word; she, in contrast, is the one who twice blesses Mary, is the first to acknowledge that Mary is "the mother of the Lord," is the one who is the focus of rejoicing of neighbors and relatives (1:58), and is the one who gives the name to the child (1:60), a name that in the narrative has been revealed only to Zechariah, who cannot speak. Although Elizabeth is gone from the scene as soon as the child "grows and becomes strong in spirit," she nonetheless plays an important role as a wise woman who can perceive the pattern of God's salvation, like the prophetess Anna (2:36–38).

Similarly, Mary plays a much more active role in chapter 1 than she does in the rest of the birth narratives in Luke, even though she is depicted as the submissive "slave of the Lord." As in the three revelation episodes, Mary wants to know what is meant by Gabriel's words: "She was much perplexed by his words and pondered what sort of greeting this might be" (1:29). She also wants to know *how* it is to be accomplished: "How can this be, since I do not know a man?" (1:34). Only then does she consent to the "word" spoken by Gabriel, the possible impossible. In her song of praise in 1:46–55, Mary recapitulates the salvation history of Israel in such a way that she acknowledges her role in it: "Surely from now on all generations will call me blessed" (1:48, NRSV). These are the words of a wise woman, a woman who surely knows both her own role and that of the child to be born to her, as did Elizabeth, who acknowledged Jesus in the womb as "the Lord." In the three subsequent revelation episodes (2:17–19; 2:34–35; and 2:48–51), Mary's knowledge and perception are represented as waning. In the scene at the manger in Bethlehem, while others are "amazed" at the revelation of the shepherds, Mary "puts these words together" in her heart, just as she did the greeting of Gabriel. She asks no questions. Similarly, when Simeon delivers to her the rather cryptic prophecy about the sword that will pierce her soul, she asks no questions. In the last episode, Jesus' wisdom and understanding are contrasted with Mary's lack of understanding (2:50). Mary no longer "ponders" these things but keeps them "in her heart" (2:51). I suggest that Luke is deliberately downplaying Mary's role because of her prominence in the earlier narratives, which he adapted to his own scheme of salvation history. In these narratives, even as they presently appear in Luke, Mary (along with Elizabeth) is perceptive, even questioning, and wise. As a "mother in Israel," she might be expected to fulfill the role of instructor in saving wisdom in the household. Since Jesus, not Mary, is the savior of Israel, her role as instructress is deliberately undercut by Luke and shifted to Jesus as instructor in the episode in which he is found in the Temple. Further, just as the community that produced Q, which Luke uses as a source, both denigrated the role of women as biological mothers and rejected the mother of the household as an embodiment of wisdom, so also Luke reduces Mary's role as biological mother and downplays her role as wise woman and even as disciple. Perhaps Mary was in danger of "getting away" from Luke, of detracting from his portrayal of Jesus as the fulcrum of salvation history.

Mary plays a similar paradoxical role in the Gospel of John. On the one hand, she appears in two significant places: at the beginning of Jesus' ministry, with the first "sign" (*semeion*—miracle) at Cana in 2:1–12, and at the end of Jesus' ministry, at the foot of the cross (19:25–27). On the other hand, she is never mentioned specifically by her name, only as "the mother of Jesus" or "Jesus' mother,"[33] and the two scenes in which she does have a part seem deliberately designed, either by the evangelist or a later editor, to dissociate Jesus not only from the act of physical birth, but from his biological mother. Once again, for John as for Luke, Mary appears to be the means by which the word became flesh, by which the spiritual became physical, but the evangelist does not wish to dwell upon the process. For John, Jesus, like all the true children of God, takes his origin "from above": He is "born [begotten], not of blood, nor of the will of the flesh, nor of the will of a man [*aner*, male], but of God" (John 1:13). John, like Mark, does not dwell upon the birth or upon the infancy of Jesus: for him, Jesus is the "stranger from heaven," come like Wisdom down to earth to call "his own" from the world to heaven, whence he came and will return. The process by which this heavenly Logos "became flesh" (1:14) does not really interest John: "John was not interested in the mother of Jesus as the mother of

the messiah king . . . since the Johannine Jesus is the messianic son of God not because of his earthly birth from
Mary but because of his heavenly pre-existence with the
father."[34]

Indeed, what distinguishes those who "have knowledge" in the Gospel of John is that they can recognize
not only Jesus' true birth, but their own. In John's version of the rejection of Jesus by his own people, following
the miracle of bread from heaven (see Mark 6:1–6a),
"the Jews" (his people of earthly origin) think that they
"know" where he comes from: "Is not this Jesus, the son
of Joseph? Do we not know his father and his mother?
How does he now say, 'I have come down from heaven'?"
(John 6:42, NRSV). Jesus' response refers to "the Father," namely God, who has sent him (6:43–51) as the
true "bread from heaven." These same or similar opponents again talk about true, legitimate parentage, which
in John is a way of talking about origins, in the controversy about the "children of Abraham" in 8:39–58. Jesus'
opponents have claimed they are children of Abraham,
but he has retorted that they act not like Abraham, the
father they claim, but like "their father," who Jesus later
says is the devil (8:44). In a possible allusion to charges
of Jesus' illegitimate birth, they reply, "We are not illegitimate children [born of fornication]. We have one father,
God himself" (8:41). Through this exchange, it is clear
that if God were truly their father, they would recognize
Jesus' true birth and true origin: "If God were your Father, you would love me, for I came from God and now
am here. I did not come on my own, but he sent me.
Why do you not understand what I say? It is because
you cannot receive my word" (8:42–43, NRSV, modified).
Like all questions of origin in the Gospel of John, this dialogue points only to Jesus as the manifestation of God in
the world, the Logos who has been sent from above. For
such a figure, physical birth has little importance: "What
is born of the flesh is flesh, and what is born of the Spirit
is spirit" (3:5). Even Jesus' own (earthly) brothers do not

recognize who he truly is: They press him to perform "works" to "show yourself to the world" (7:3–4), because "not even his brothers believed in him" (7:5).

In the episode of the miracle at Cana, the first "sign" in which Jesus' "glory" is revealed (2:11), and at which his "disciples believed in him," Jesus' mother appears to belong to those, like his brothers and Nicodemus, who do not perceive his glory and do not "know" fully who Jesus is. This categorizing of Jesus' mother among those who misunderstand him is not unlike her portrayal by Mark. Hence, in John, as in Mark, there are no divine pronouncements as to the identity of the child his mother is to bear. Instead, there is a distinct distancing, even of the birth of Jesus, from Mary. This distancing in John seems particularly clear, and even a shade polemical, in the two episodes in which Mary figures, the first being the wedding at Cana. In Robert Fortna's reconstruction of this event as it first appeared in the "Gospel of Signs," the putative source from which John derived the miracles of Jesus, the "mother of Jesus" is present, along with Jesus and his disciples, as in the current text (John 2:1–2). But, when the wine gives out, Jesus' mother merely observes to the servants, "Do whatever he tells you" (2:5).[35] There is no dialogue between Jesus and his mother and no harsh retort, as in the present John 2:3–4: "When the wine gave out, the mother of Jesus said to him, 'They have no wine.' And Jesus said to her, 'Woman, what is that between you and me? My hour has not yet come.' His mother said to the servants, 'Do whatever he tells you'" (NRSV).

Much has been written about this episode, mostly in an attempt to explain away Jesus' harshness to his mother. The comparison of the present text with its earlier version, however, suggests some possibilities that recognize Jesus' retort for what it is: a rebuke to Mary. Jesus' addressing his mother as "Woman" (*gyne*) is not polite; nor is it an address that has any precedent in Hebrew or Greek "for a son to his mother."[36] This form of address

is doubly significant. In the first place, Jesus addresses
all other women in this Gospel in this manner, including
the Samaritan woman (4:21), whom one might expect he
would not address in the most polite manner. Thus, Jesus
"places no special emphasis on [Mary's] physical motherhood," merely categorizing her with other women, who
may or may not understand his true nature.[37] In the second place, Jesus again addresses Mary as "Woman" at
the foot of the cross (19:25–27), where he assigns her a
"son," the beloved disciple. Once again, Jesus dissociates
himself from his physical mother: He is no longer her
son because his "hour" has indeed come; he is returning to his Father, from whom he came. Mary's physical
motherhood, at the cross as at Cana, means nothing in
terms of John's spiritual Gospel. A further dissociation
may be seen in the rebuke at Cana, where Jesus replies
to his mother's remark about there being no wine. Mary
apparently knows enough of her son's powers to expect
him to do something, and yet he retorts: "What is that
between you and me [*ti emoi kai soi*]?" It is hard to convey
the harshness of the wording in English, but the sense of
it is that there is no connection between Mary and Jesus:
There is *nothing* between them such that her concerns
should have anything to do with him. Mary, as Jesus'
mother, may not expect anything of him: Any "hour" for
his manifestation as messiah or glorification as the Son of
God is to be a matter between his heavenly Father and
him, and has nothing to do with his mother. She is not
even included in those disciples who "believed in him"
after the miracle (2:11). The fact that he *does* perform the
miracle, apparently at her request, indirect though it may
be, results from the narrative in the source, modified by
the evangelist to include the rebuke to Mary; it does not
make it "virtually impossible to maintain that the scene
contains a harsh polemic against his mother."[38] On the
contrary, the evangelist has probably modified his source
material to *include* such a polemic.
It appears, then, that both of the episodes directly in-

volving Mary in John's Gospel, while acknowledging that Jesus does have an earthly, physical mother, deliberately distance him from that mother as far as is possible, while still acknowledging her existence and her presence, at the beginning and end of Jesus' ministry. As Raymond E. Brown has noted, "The Fourth Gospel agrees with the other three that Mary had no role in the ministry as Jesus' physical mother."[39] However, I do not believe that John's Gospel thereby shows Mary to have been included among the "true" disciples, those who recognize Jesus as embodying the word and the will of God (see Mark 3:31–35 and parallels), or even to have been the "spiritual" mother of the community of the beloved disciple.[40] Mary does not even appear as one of the witnesses of the empty tomb: Mary Magdalene is the sole first witness, and the first to see the risen Jesus. It is thus hard to perceive Mary, Jesus' mother, as included among the disciples and as having "grown" in perception along the way: After all, she only appears twice. I believe, rather, that either the evangelist or possibly a later redactor from the Johannine community needed to emphasize the fact that Jesus *had* a physical mother because of possible Docetist tendencies arising in the community as a result of its high Christology.[41] Such tendencies seemed to emphasize Jesus' birth from the Spirit rather than the flesh (1 John 4:1–3), a viewpoint to which the Gospel in its earlier stages certainly must have contributed (e.g., John 1:13; 3:6). Nevertheless, while showing that Jesus did have a mother, the evangelist or redactor seems to have definitely dissociated him from her as much as possible, almost as if she interrupted the grand pattern of the descent, rejection, and ultimate ascent of the heavenly Logos. Why this reluctance? I suggest two possibilities: first, that the Johannine community, in common with other Christian communities, even the earliest ones, had rejected motherhood, both as a desirable role for women, especially women disciples, and because it was a reminder of physicality and location in this world; second, that

Mary as Jesus' mother had perhaps a greater role in some Christian communities than would appear from the evidence of the canonical New Testament. Since an examination of Mary in the noncanonical writings of the late first to early third centuries would show whether she was deliberately excluded from the canon for some polemical purpose, it is to these noncanonical writings that we must now turn.

"A Thing That Nature Does Not Allow": Mary Outside the Canon

Like the Gospels that later became part of the New Testament canon, the extracanonical gospels stand at the end of a process of oral transmission. Like the canonical Gospels also, the apocryphal materials served the theological interests of certain Christian communities, communities that were only later recognized as heterodox by the increasingly orthodox church, especially in the West. Some of the Eastern churches, particularly the Semitic Christian ones, had little difficulty with female imagery and female aspects of the divine, following both the "instinct of grammar," in which both the Holy Spirit and Wisdom were feminine, and "inherited religious thought patterns," which gave prominence to mother goddesses like the Dea Syria, Cybele, and Isis.[42] It is probably no accident then that the Christian communities of the Syrian Orient produced literature like the *Odes of Solomon,* which contains strong female imagery and in which a female Holy Spirit plays a prominent role, and also the Gnostic scriptures belonging to the Thomas tradition, in which Sophia, female Wisdom, has a role. The Thomas tradition and related Gnostic traditions were also transmitted to Egypt, where they probably influenced, or at least intersected with, the writings of the Christian Gnostic teacher Valentinus and his followers, who produced *The Gospel of Philip*.[43] But not just Gnostic traditions were popular in the East: Syriac-speaking churches preserved and perhaps generated traditions about Mary, devotion to whom was stronger and more highly developed at an earlier point in time (the fourth century) than it was in the West.[44]

Such traditions included the most popular and influential of the noncanonical traditions, a gospel that is actually the story of Mary from her own birth to that of Jesus, the *Protevangelium of James*, which is linked in Syriac manuscripts to the story of Mary's death, the *Transitus Mariae*, or *Passing of Mary*. Further interest in Mary of a more popular sort was evidenced by the Syriac *Life of the Virgin* or *History of the Blessed Virgin*, which included miracles performed by Mary herself. In short, as Susan Ashbrook Harvey has observed, "Mary's place in early Syriac Christianity was not regarded with the doctrinal reservations and inhibitions expressed further west before the fifth century."[45] It appears also as though Marian devotion was strong in Byzantine popular religion; that devotion was channeled and used to advantage by the church authorities in declaring Mary the *Theotokos*, thc "God-bearer," at the First Council of Ephesus, in 431. A fragmentary prayer for Mary's intercession appears in a Greek papyrus, perhaps from the third or fourth century, and may reflect this popular devotion. Obviously modified from the Our Father, it beseeches Mary: "Mother of God [hear] my supplications: suffer us not [to be] in adversity, but deliver us from danger."[46] It is tempting, but impossible, to link this kind of prayer to the practices of the Thracian-descended Arabian women whose devotion to the Virgin Mary so scandalized Epiphanius in the fourth century: "They prepare a kind of cake in the name of the ever-Virgin, assemble together, and in the name of the holy Virgin they attempt to undertake a deed that is irrev-

erent and blasphemous beyond measure—in her name
they function as priests for women" (Epiphanius, *Medicine Box* 78.23).[47] What could not be properly channeled
by the ecclesiastical and temporal authorities, therefore,
became known as heresy. Similarly, Pope Gelasius I (492–
496) in the West condemned the *Protevangelium of James,*
circulated in its Latin version as *Pseudo-Matthew,* and also
condemned the *Passing of Mary* and other similar infancy
gospels, although he and others were not successful in
suppressing such material, which had caught the popular
imagination.[48]

What was it about the Virgin Mother Mary that ap-
pealed to this imagination, and, judging from the example cited by Epiphanius, the female popular imagination particularly? And why did the increasingly orthodox
church, particularly in the West, both channel and sup-
press this Marian devotion, at least in its initial stages?
The answer to the second question in a sense lies in the
answer to the first: Popular religiosity, especially that of
women, was always a source of concern to the authorities in antiquity, be they pagan, Jewish, or Christian. In
the latter two cases, any devotion directed away from
the one (male) deity and toward another was apostasy.
Judaism managed to incarnate the female Hokhmah as
the Torah, the object of study by male sages; Christianity
incarnated the female Sophia as the male Logos in the
male Christ, who was the sole manifestation of God. In
the Greek-speaking churches, the Holy Spirit itself was
lexically neuter (*pneuma*), rather than feminine (Hebrew
ruach; Syriac *ruha'*). This evidence might support the the-
sis that Mary existed in popular piety because that piety
needed a female deity or at least some female aspect to
the deity that seemed so exclusively male. In Rosemary R.
Ruether's words, "Masses of people who came into the
Christian church brought with them their former devotion to the mother goddess," especially the goddess Isis,
whose iconography was borrowed to represent Mary.[49]
Ruether distinguishes this "popular piety"—which con-

nected Mary's feasts with those of earth goddesses and generated tales like those in the apocryphal gospels that transformed her into a "substitute mother goddess"— from that being developed by the clerics and monastics, who praised Mary as the "new Eve," the "docile and obedient virgin."[50] Some iconographic representations of Mary seated with the infant Jesus on her lap suggest representations of Isis with the infant Horus, as do the crescent moon and stars, also linked to Isis but adapted to fit Mary as the childbearing "woman clothed with the sun" in Revelation 12:1–6. Hilda Graef also points to imagery in the second-century *Odes of Solomon* that suggests Mary's bearing herself "as if she were a man, of her own will," and also depicts her as a "mother with many mercies"; this imagery appears "to fit the goddess Isis, the mother of Horus," and may be a result of syncretistic tendencies in some Christian circles.[51]

Nevertheless, it must also be noted that the iconography that links Mary to Isis is rather late (fifth century at the earliest), and emphasizes rather the infant king, Jesus, a substitute for Horus as the infant pharaoh. The link between the "woman clothed with the sun" and Mary was made by some persons at some time prior to Epiphanius in the fourth century, but the figure was mainly identified as the church, the mother of the faithful.[52] The crescent moon, which as a symbol of Isis was itself borrowed from the iconography of the Egyptian Hathor and the Greek Artemis, ended up in Marian iconography probably as a result of the passage in Revelation 12:1–6, and not as a direct borrowing from Isis. In all representations of Isis, the crescent moon is on her head (a modification of Hathor's cow horns, borrowed from her iconography), whereas it appears beneath the feet of the woman in Revelation 12 and in all representations of Mary. But these are minor points compared to the major difficulty in seeing popular devotion to Mary as resulting from a simple identification of her with another mother goddess. This difficulty is pointed out by Michael P. Carroll in *The Cult of the Virgin Mary:*

> It is very tempting to see Mary as simply the latest in a long line of mother goddesses who have dominated Mediterranean religions over the past several millennia. This would be a mistake. Although there are similarities, Mary is quite different from almost all earlier mother goddesses in at least one very important way: she is completely dissociated from sexuality.[53]

Although there were certainly goddesses in the Greco-Roman world who were both virgin and mother, Isis being an example, Artemis/Diana of Ephesus (see Acts 19) being another, the process of dissociating virginity from motherhood took place sooner and more often in Greco-Roman myth and religion than Carroll assumes, the bifurcation of Demeter-Kore, the mother-maiden pair of the Eleusinian mysteries, being an ancient example. It may be that such a bifurcation went on in Christian circles, particularly of the heterodox variety, in the figures of Mary (Jesus' mother) and Mary Magdalene (see *Gospel of Philip* 59.5–10). Nevertheless, Carroll is correct in his observation that the emphasis on Mary as a virgin mother, whether in orthodox or heterodox Christianity, falls almost completely on her virginity and her nonphysical motherhood, the latter of which was emphasized even as early as the canonical gospels, although the noncanonical materials, particularly the *Protevangelium of James,* lay much more emphasis on her complete virginity. Let us attempt to see: (1) why Mary's virginity and spiritual, nonphysical motherhood were so necessary, both to the theology of the orthodox and to the popular and heterodox materials; (2) if these aspects of Mary were necessary for different reasons; and (3) how they related to the lives and practices of women within the circles that produced both types of literature.

In the Gnostic literature that now is identified with

the Nag Hammadi Library, there is much about motherhood, and much of that is negative. In several versions of Gnostic myth and theology, the physical motherhood of Sophia (Wisdom), as we have seen, results in a creation that is material, physical, and botched, filled with the ignorance that is death. Gnostic Christianity, like many varieties of Christianity in the first and second centuries of its existence, tended to be severely ascetic and even Encratitic. Many Gnostic Christians did not believe that Jesus Christ had a truly physical or material body, so the physical motherhood of Mary became problematic. The *Gospel of Thomas* is a compilation of the "secret" teachings of Jesus as divine Wisdom; it is related to the Synoptic Gospels and Q and originated in Gnostic Christian circles in northern Mesopotamia. In that work Jesus' mother, Mary, occupies a place similar to that in the Synoptic Gospels: That is, her position as mother is not as important as her position among Jesus' disciples. The *Gospel of Thomas* preserves the Synoptic saying of Jesus on his "true family" consisting of those who "do the will of my Father" (*Gospel of Thomas* 49.21–25; parallels in Matt. 12:47; Mark 3:32; Luke 8:20), and two versions of the Synoptic saying on hating one's biological family (42.25–27; parallels in Matt. 10:37; Luke 14:26; *Gospel of Thomas* 49.32–50.1). The second version of this saying in the *Gospel of Thomas*, unfortunately fragmentary, like many Gnostic sayings, contains a paradox: "[Jesus said], 'Those who do not hate their [father] and their mother as I do cannot be [disciples] of me. And those who [do not] love their [father and] their mother as I do cannot be [disciples of] me. For my mother [. . .] But my true [mother] gave me life' " (49.32–50.1).[54] Apparently, there is a distinction being made between the "true" parents, who are spiritual, and the "apparent" earthly parents, who are mere flesh, Jesus' "true mother" perhaps being interpreted as the Holy Spirit or Wisdom. The only other saying in the *Gospel of Thomas* relating to Jesus' mother, Mary, is a version of the pronouncement of blessing on Jesus' mother, found in Luke 11:27, possibly combined with the Lukan prediction of the destruction of Jerusalem in Luke 23:28 (*Gospel of Thomas* 47.3–11). Once again, the emphasis is shifted away from physical motherhood and toward spiritual motherhood, the production of disciples who do the Father's will.

These sayings as they are contained in *Thomas* are consistent with the view of the Thomaic Christians that spiritual birth is important, and that physical birth is not merely unimportant—it belongs to the material realm and is therefore not real or "true." Logion 105 (50.16), for example, sums up this point of view: "Jesus said, 'Whoever is acquainted with the[ir] father and the[ir] mother will be called the offspring of a prostitute.' "[55] Salvation is achieved only by spiritual unity, in which the female component, representing physicality for the most part, is either distinctly inferior or absorbed by the male. In the often-cited Logion 114, Jesus responds to Peter's complaint that Mary (Magdalene) cannot be a disciple since "females are not worthy of [the] life." Jesus states: "See, I am going to attract her to make her male so that she too might become a living spirit that resembles you males. For every female (element) that makes itself male will enter the kingdom of heavens" (51.18–24).[56] Salvation, then, is "making the two one" and the "male and the female one and the same" (Logion 22; *Gospel of Thomas* 37.24), but expressed in such a way that they metaphorically become "male": that is, animate spirit. Physicality, including the means by which physical bodies get into the world, is left behind.

The Valentinian, Gnostic Christian *Gospel of Philip* consists of sayings and pronouncements anthologized from other works. It was probably put together some time in the early to middle third century, although the works it anthologizes may have originated in the second century.[57] In the work, Mary, Jesus' mother, plays a somewhat less negative role than she does in the *Gospel of Thomas*. Because some of the sayings appear to reflect a Syriac origin, it is probable that they belong to the "eastern" branch of Gnostic Christianity, from the Syrian Orient. In Logion 14 (55.23–31), for example, the Holy Spirit is conceived of as female (as in Semitic languages), and a pronouncement is made upon the impossibility of Mary's conceiving by the Spirit:

> Some said that Mary conceived by the holy spirit: they are mistaken, they do not realize what they say. When did a female ever conceive by a female? Mary is the virgin whom the forces [powers] did not defile. Her existence is anathema to the Hebrews, meaning the apostles and apostolic persons. This virgin whom the forces did not defile [. . .] forces defiled them(selves?).[58]

This saying reflects two traditions common to the Valentinians and other Gnostics, particularly the Sethians: first, that physical conception resulted from a rape of the physical woman, Eve, by the "powers" or "forces" of this world and was therefore to be avoided (see *Apocryphon of John* 24.8–32; *Hypostasis of the Archons* 89.17–29; 92.18–93.1, where the "virgin whom the powers did not defile" is Norea, Seth's female counterpart); and second, that Mary was the "pure vessel" through whom the spiritual Jesus emerged into the world, either as an animate body or a spiritual essence (see *Gospel of the Egyptians* 74.25–29; Irenaeus, *Against Heresies* 1.30.12). In both cases, Mary's complete virginity, free from any taint of sexual intercourse, makes her fit to be the pure (spiritual) vessel through whom the savior appears in the world. Apparently, this Logion from the *Gospel of Philip* is intended as a polemic, either against the "apostles" (orthodox) and those who follow them, who do not understand the true nature of Jesus' birth, or against other Gnostics who claim that the Spirit descended on Mary in Jesus' conception, not upon the animate Jesus at his baptism, a thing that would be impossible if one saw the Spirit as female.[59] Epiphanius, in his polemic against the Gnostic

Phibionites, who may be a branch of the Valentinians, alleges that they claim Jesus was "not born of Mary but manifested by Mary" (*Medicine Box* 26.20.5). In either case, the spiritual savior comes into the world through female agency, which redeems the physical aspect of creation that originated as the end result of the disastrous conception of Sophia or her lower counterpart, Sophia Prounikos (see *Gospel of Philip* 60.10–12). A slightly different version of this act of redemption is stated in 71.16: Because Adam "came into being from two virgins, the Holy Spirit and the virgin earth," Christ "was born from a virgin to rectify the fall which occurred in the beginning."[60] Mary, the mother of Jesus, is linked not only to the Holy Spirit as a spiritual mother, but also to the other Marys with whom Jesus is associated: Mary Magdalene and his sister (Mary) (59.6–10). As such, "Mary" is his "companion" and his "partner" (the female part of the syzygy), and thus may also represent Sophia as his partner and companion.[61] Her role is thus once again dissociated with physical motherhood and associated with discipleship and spiritual companionship: The female is incomplete as a mother without the male.

Among Gnostic Christians, as we saw in the case of Sophia, when motherhood is envisioned as physical, connected with the conception and procreation of material bodies, it is denigrated. Mary as Jesus' mother therefore has little role in the Gnostic scheme of salvation, overshadowed as she is, first by the figure of Sophia, sometimes by the Holy Spirit, then by the disciple, Mary Magdalene; and, as we have seen above, she is on occasion identified with all three. In other words, her role is symbolic. As regards Mary specifically as the mother of the savior, the only texts that appear to accord her any kind of importance are those, usually Valentinian and Sethian, that view her as a "pure vessel," incontrovertibly virgin, who was not defiled by the act of intercourse and who passed nothing physical, nothing material, especially not a body, to Jesus. Irenaeus charged the Valentinians with saying and believing that Jesus "passed through Mary like water through a tube" (*Against Heresies* 1.7.2). Other Gnostic Christians denied that Christ had any involvement with Mary at all: For example, *3 Corinthians* 1.14 states quite succinctly that heretics believe "the Lord is not come in the flesh, nor was he born of Mary."[62] The later followers of the Persian syncretistic religion of Mani (216–277), who combined Gnostic Christianity with Zoroastrianism and Buddhism, totally rejected the idea of Christ coming in the flesh, particularly female flesh. Mani states, "Far be it from me that I should confess our Lord Jesus Christ to have come down through the natural reproductive organs of a woman. For he himself gives witness that he descended from the bosom of the Father."[63] This denial of the actual human birth of Christ, as we shall see, was the reason for the patristic writers' concentration on the humanity of Christ being derived from his mother Mary, albeit in a way that avoided the "uncleanness of women" (Epiphanius, *Medicine Box* 66.6.9).

The *Protevangelium of James*—written in the first half of the second century but perhaps embodying much earlier traditions—offers an alternative to the Gnostic and orthodox Christian interpretation of Mary; the work was certainly influential on the latter, while it had ties to the former. Like the orthodox and heterodox interest in Mary, that of the *Protevangelium* centers upon the virginity of Mary—that is, upon the virginal conception and virgin birth of Jesus. Mentioned by both Origen and Clement of Alexandria, this book, written "for the glorification of Mary,"[64] does not belong to the Gnostics; nor was it ever accepted as canonical by the orthodox, although elements in it—such as the perpetual virginity of Mary and the immaculate conception of Mary (i.e., her exemption from original sin) by her parents—have become over the years accepted as dogma, particularly in the Western Catholic church. The *Protevangelium* is also useful to the historian of Mary, in that it provides some evidence that, by at least 150, there was a growth in de-

votion to Mary herself, such that an entire "gospel" was
composed in which her life and her own virginal conception were made parallel to those of Christ. It is also
related to those circles that produced the apocryphal
(noncanonical) Acts, in that it places a high value on
virginity and especially upon female virginity, such that
Mary becomes the model for Christian virgins.

In the *Protevangelium,* the purported author, James
(Jesus' brother in the canonical Gospels), relates the story
of Mary's parents, Joachim and Anna, whose elderly bar-
renness and their despair of a child echo the Lukan birth
narrative of John the Baptist, itself modeled upon the
conceptions of Isaac and Samuel. Mary's birth is the occasion for a brief "magnificat" (*Protevangelium* 5.2: "My
soul is magnified this day" [see Luke 1:46]), while the
child Mary, like Jesus, daily "grows strong" (6.1; see
Luke 2:40) and is dedicated in the Temple. She also
is blessed by the "chief priests and scribes and elders
and the whole people of Israel," who give her a "name
renowned forever among all generations" (6:2; see Luke
1:48). In her dedication to the Temple, which recalls that
of Samuel and Jesus, Mary is placed "among the undefiled daughters of the Hebrews" and is blessed by the
priest, who praises the Lord for having "magnified your
name among all generations: because of you the Lord
at the end of days will manifest his redemption to the
children of Israel." The passage recalls the blessing of
Simeon on the child Jesus (7.2; see Luke 2:29–32) and
the Magnificat (Luke 1:46–55). Miraculously, the child
Mary in the Temple is nurtured by food from an angel
"like a dove," a symbol recalling the Holy Spirit that rests
on Jesus in his baptism in Luke, signifying his birth from
God (8.1; see Luke 2:22). Mary's marriage to Joseph is
brought about by a "miraculous sign," and the annun-
ciation of the virgin birth is repeated almost verbatim
from Luke 1:26–38, with a significant alteration: Mary
questions whether she shall "bear as every woman bears"
(11.2–3), which of course she will not; Jesus' birth will

be a spiritual birth, and not of the ordinary kind. When Mary is in her sixth month of pregnancy, Joseph, who has not had intercourse with her, berates himself for the "evil" that has happened to "defile" the "virgin out of the Temple," questioning whether the "story of Adam" has been repeated, since "the serpent found Eve alone and deceived her and defiled her" (13.1), a variant of the Eve/Mary typology. At this point, the *Protevangelium* appears to reconcile the birth narratives of Luke and Matthew because an announcement is made to Joseph, who decides not to divorce Mary for adultery (Matt. 1:20–24). Mary and Joseph, indicted by the scribe Annas, are forced to drink the *sotah* (the bitter water used in Judaism to detect an adulterous woman) in the wilderness, replicating the temptation story of Jesus (16.1–2). The rest of the story follows the birth narrative of Luke fairly closely, until Mary gives birth to Jesus. Joseph finds a midwife, who pronounces, upon seeing a "dark bright cloud" overshadowing the cave in which Mary is lying, "My soul is magnified today, for my eyes have seen wonderful things, for salvation is born to Israel" (19.2; see Luke 2:30–32). The midwife then testifies to Salome, who appears in other extracanonical works as one of Jesus' disciples (e.g., *Gospel of Thomas* 43.23–33), that "a virgin has brought forth, a thing which (her) nature does not allow." Salome, like Thomas in John 20:25, doubts the veracity of this testimony and stretches forth her finger to test Mary's virginity after birth: It promptly withers, and is only restored miraculously by the infant (20.3–4).

In extant noncanonical literature, the pregospel of James (*Protevangelium of James*) is unique: We have no other gospel, canonical or noncanonical, that so emphasizes the virginity of Mary before, during, and after birth (*ante partum, in partu,* and *ex partu*). The Latin version of this narrative, Pseudo-Matthew, appears to have been quite popular in the West until its condemnation under Pope Gelasius I. Nevertheless, Jerome, who was instrumental in its condemnation, is alleged to have written

that "whether these stories be true or inventions, the sacred nativity of St. Mary was preceded by great miracles,
and succeeded by the greatest."[65] The *Transitus Mariae*
(*Passing of Mary*) that accompanies the *Protevangelium* in
some of the manuscripts also emphasizes Mary's virginity
and her assumption into heaven, paralleling the ascent of
Jesus to heaven in Acts 1:9–11. In this version, Jesus himself calls her "blessed mother, queen of all the saints," and
Joseph (alleged in the Latin version to be the author) calls
her the "most sacred temple" of the Lord, "the blessed
Mary ever-virgin."[66] In the Syriac cycle of miracles related
to Mary and the infant Jesus, miracles are performed by
the use of the water in which Jesus is washed, or with
his swaddling bands, or even by suckling the breast of
Mary, an act through which the resurrection of the infant
Thomas Didymus is effected.[67] In this same narrative, *The
History of the Blessed Virgin,* there is even a messianic-secret
motif in which Mary cautions each person healed at her
direction to tell no one.

Clearly, these noncanonical stories, scant though they
may be, reveal traditions about Mary, about her relationship to Jesus, and about her prominent role as a
miracle worker. These traditions developed and continued in the second through the fourth centuries, perhaps
alongside those that are now embodied in the canonical Gospels and Acts. Rather than concentrating upon
Jesus, powerful even in infancy as the savior, they con-
centrate upon the figure of Mary and her power *as* the
virgin mother. It is probable that such gospels as the *Protevangelium of James,* while influential in orthodox theology,
were not accepted into the canon for two reasons: the
concentration on Mary rather than Jesus as the source
of the miracle (as she is the "source" of Jesus), and the
strong emphasis on her ascetic virginity, which seems to
provide her with miracle-working power. The latter is
consistent with other apocryphal Christian materials of
the same time period, the second to the fourth centuries,
in which virginal or celibate women (Thecla in *Acts of The-*

cla; Mygdonia in *Acts of Thomas;* Drusilla in *Acts of John*)
separate from their betrothed or husbands and acquire
miracle-working power and authority *because* of their virginal or celibate life-style.[68] Therefore, there seems to be
a connection between the acquisition of divine power and
virginity, or refusal to exercise female sexuality.

Thus far, we have seen that in the noncanonical Gnostic and other heterodox writings, Mary has a prominent
role only when one of two factors is emphasized: her virginity or the lack of physicality when she conceived and
gave birth to Jesus. The emphasis on Mary's virginity, like
that in the Gospels of Matthew and Luke, cannot be entirely the function of an apologetic against the charge of
Jesus' illegitimate birth, however it may have originated.
Mary's virginity and its connection with the divine power
that effects salvation have another function, a function
that relates to the way in which the conception and childbearing of women within the early Christian world was
viewed, both by women themselves and by the shapers
of the New Testament canon, the church fathers. In the
writings of the latter, who increasingly denied women
equal formal partnership in the Christian communities,
the typology of Eve/Mary appears to have prevailed and
to have formed a framework within which women and
their role in the economy of salvation were envisioned.

"Saved by Childbearing": Mothers or Virgins?

In the first epistle to Timothy, probably dating
around the beginning of the second century C.E. (ca. 125),
the writer assigns a positive value to the household (*oikia*)
as managed in the Roman patriarchal system familiar to

the author by the *pater* and *mater familias* (1 Tim. 3:1–
13). Those who are to be bishops (*episkopoi*), an office
reserved in 1 Timothy for men, and those to be deacons
(*diakonoi*), an office apparently open to both men and
women (3:8–13), are to replicate within the congregation the sound management desired in their households.
In contrast, married women within the congregation are
now adjured to "dress modestly and decently" and to
"learn in silence with full submission." The author allows
no woman to "teach or hold authority over a man," giving as his reasons the deception of Eve before Adam, a
rare and early instance of the use of Eve's transgression
to justify the subordination of women within the Christian churches, and an expansion on the order of creation
in Paul's first letter to the Corinthians (1 Cor. 11:2–16).
The text in Timothy states: "For Adam was formed first,
then Eve; and Adam was not deceived, but the woman
[*gyne;* a word that can also mean 'wife'] was deceived and
became a transgressor" (1 Tim. 2:13–14, NRSV). Clearly
the instructions here are to married women, and just as
clearly the author believes that the transgression of the
progenitress Eve can be nullified and her female descen-
dants redeemed if women behave "properly": "Yet she
will be saved through childbearing, provided they continue in faith and love and holiness, with modesty" (2:15,
NRSV). The unusual shift in pronouns, from the feminine
singular to the feminine plural, may invite some to think
that by "childbearing" (which in the Greek has a definite
article, "the childbearing") is meant the bearing of Jesus
by Mary. However, such an interpretation is based rather
too hopefully on doctrinal considerations and on reading patristic authors' consistent identification of Eve and
Mary back into the text of 1 Timothy. The definite article is probably not significant since it is also used with
many other nouns (e.g., "the god," *ho theos*). The change
from the singular to the plural initially ties all women
to Eve ("the woman") and then specifies the Christian
women of the congregation, who are expected not only to

be saved by their bearing children, but also to continue acting as befits honorable Christian wives. This state is recommended also for younger widows (5:14–15), so that they may not "turn away to follow Satan," busy as they will be with bearing children and managing their households. With his emphasis on Eve's being "deceived" and his corresponding stress upon the necessity for women not to "be led astray" by Satanic teaching (5:15; see 2 Tim. 3:6–7), the author is probably employing Eve as a metaphor for the wife who is "led astray" by deceptive instruction, perhaps the instruction of those who teach "profane myths and old wives' tales" (4:7). Some of these teachings condemned by the writer of Timothy probably involved either outright Gnostic instruction or teachings on asceticism and Encratism that would instruct women to avoid marriage and its result, childbirth. These "deceitful spirits and teachings of demons," as they are referred to in Timothy, "forbid marriage" (4:1–3). Therefore, in insisting both on marriage and upon childbearing for women, the author appears to be engaging in a polemic against those women who would choose the celibate life: Even widows are encouraged to marry and bear children, if they are of the childbearing age (5:14).

If we can assume that Gnosticism and other forms of heterodoxy were present in Christian circles in the early second century, then it would certainly seem that some Christian women, following the Gnostic teachings, would have eschewed marriage and childbearing. Indeed, by emphasizing childbearing as the foremost factor in women's salvation (or at least the salvation of wives), the author of Timothy was opposing other paths to salvation, paths that may have been preferred by women. Judging from the apocryphal Acts, in which every female character, even if she is married at the beginning of the story, shuns sexual intercourse, this would certainly appear to be the case. Women in the heterodox circles that produced this literature, which probably in its oral stage arose among women and may even have been written by women to praise and encourage virginity and celibacy, seem definitely to have preferred the freedom from marriage and certainly from the pains and dangers of childbearing that the ascetic life-style gave them. It also gave them some measure of autonomy and authority, as is shown in dramatic form in the *Acts of Thecla,* which so irritated Tertullian that he pointed to the very passage in 1 Timothy discussed above as proof of the heterodox nature of the Acts.[69] Even the much-praised martyr and author Perpetua (writing in her autobiography, which was later edited, possibly by Tertullian) puts her faith above obligations to parents, to household, and to her nursing infant. In the dream in which she defeats "the adversary"—the very Satan that 1 Timothy warns will seduce women—Perpetua becomes a male gladiator. Thus it is clear that a significant number of women, most considered heterodox by second-century writers like the author of Timothy, chose celibacy over marriage, pregnancy, and childbirth, as the preferred Christian life-style.

Where did this leave the unique figure of Mary? Did early Christian women revere her as a symbol of virginity or motherhood? The Christian patriarchs often told these women that the pain of childbirth was the "curse of Eve," a suffering that was viewed, at least in part, not only as punishment but as a form of "redemption," as paying the price of Eve's misconduct in seeking wisdom that was denied her and in acting on her own. Did early Christian women view Eve as one who transcended the pain in childbirth that they themselves experienced? Or was she, as Beatrice Beaulieu has suggested, a symbolic "solution," a "both/and" answer to the problem of immanence and transcendence?[70] It is easier to see how certain ascetic women in early Christianity viewed the positive value of virginity, if their concerns are truly reflected in the apocryphal Acts and gospels, than it is to find what their attitude was toward Mary, since all extant *written* sources mentioning Mary, including most probably the laudatory *Protevangelium of James,* are by male authors. The vision of the second-century Montanist prophetess Maximilla, in which Christ appeared "in the form of a woman, radiantly robed," to "implant wisdom" in her, is nevertheless a vision of Christ, not Mary (Epiphanius, *Medicine Box* 49.1.3).

We know of only one instance, mentioned by Epiphanius in the fourth century (who quotes 1 Tim. 4:1 in his polemic against it), in which Christian women, acting as priestesses "in the name of the holy Virgin," bake cakes (a traditional offering to mother goddesses as the "queens of heaven") and offer them "in the name of the ever-Virgin," in a service that appears to be modeled on the eucharist (Epiphanius, *Medicine Box* 78.23; 79.1–9). In attempting to silence this "heresy," Epiphanius links it to Eve: "The whole of this deception is female; the disease comes from Eve who was long ago deceived" (79.2). Mary's "womb" was a "temple" prepared "for the incarnate activity of the Lord" (79.3), but this is not a reason to elevate her to divinity and especially is not a reason for women to exercise priestly functions. Further, "because death had come into the world through a woman," the "Master and Savior of all" chose to "rectify" the defect caused by Eve by being "born of a virginal woman" (79.9). (This ironically resembles the Gnostic vision—so abhorred by Epiphanius—in which Sophia, completed by her male "half," also rectified Eve's "defect.") It may be that Epiphanius takes the particular trajectory he does in condemning this heresy—linking it particularly to women, the "transgression" of Eve, and the seductive speech of the adulteress of Proverbs—because it had originated in Thrace and Scythia, come through Phrygia in Asia Minor, whence it reached Arabia, and seemed to have had a particular appeal for women in those locales. Epiphanius mentions Quintilla, Maximilla, and Priscilla, the Phrygian Montanists, as belonging to a similar heresy. His anxiety over the possible extent of this heresy among women is expressed in terms of his misogyny (the devil always uses women as his channels to seduce the righteous) and in his downplaying the importance of Mary by quoting John 2:4 ("Woman, what have I to do with you?") (79.4) and by polemics against the traditions of Mary's own immaculate conception, the same or similar ones as contained in the *Protevangelium* (79.5). In short, for Epiphanius, the Virgin as a virgin is to be revered: "Certainly the body of Mary was holy" (79.4). But she herself is not divine and is not to be revered above Christ: He is the incarnate God, the savior.

Such a polemic, if read from the other side, seems to indicate that these Christian women in fact regarded Mary herself as divine, and herself as the savior, in place of her son, Jesus. That they offered her cakes (and perhaps additionally bread), as well as wine ("the old mixed cup of Fortuna" [79.8]), indicates that they worshiped her in the manner traditionally appropriate to a Mediterranean mother goddess. Indeed, Epiphanius compares their worship to that of the women inveighed against by Jeremiah for worshiping the "queen of heaven" (79.8). Perhaps Epiphanius's reference to Fortune here is an indication of the possible belief by these women that Mary, like Isis, conquered Chance or Fate. Thus it may be that certain Christian women saw Mary in her role as mother as their savior, and not just as redeemer, from the "curse" laid upon them as the result of Eve's transgression. But perhaps they also worshiped her as pagan women worshiped another "queen of heaven," Isis—that is, as the transcendent mother whose experience of motherhood might help them in their own and elevate it to divinity. Iconographically, there is some slim evidence to support this speculation. In the earliest representations of Mary with the infant Jesus, she is seated upon a thronelike *sella*, and he is seated upon her lap in the same manner that the infant Horus is seated upon the "throne" of Isis's lap. Both Isis and Mary thus appear, not only as "thrones" for the infant king, but as queen mothers themselves.[71] At least one Christian woman from Egypt may have made the identification of herself as mother with Mary, carrying a long-standing identification of women with Isis over into a Christianized form. In the previously mentioned stele from the Fayyum of Egypt, dated anywhere from 500–700 C.E. (Berlin, Staatliche Museum, Inv. no. 14726), an anonymous woman sits upon a thronelike chair, nursing her infant. Two crosses have been carved on either side of the seated mother, perhaps additions to an earlier stele. Did this woman see Mary or Mary's motherhood as somehow sanctifying her own? Was the identification that women had with Isis simply Christianized in an identification with Mary? We cannot say for certain.[72] Nor can we say that popular Christianity among women appears to have venerated Mary more as mother than as Virgin, although the designation of Mary as *Theotokos,* probably driven by the popular cult of Mary that appears in the Eastern churches by the fifth century, does indicate an emphasis on her motherhood rather than her virginity.[73]

However scanty the evidence for women's veneration of Mary as mother, queen of heaven, and savior, there is still less evidence for their veneration of Mary as the model for virginity. Indeed, those women who sought virginity, celibate marriage, or celibate widowhood in increasing numbers from the second to the fourth centuries appear to have replicated the distaste of the earlier Christian communities (e.g., those that produced Q and the *Gospel of Thomas*) for the ties of motherhood and for traditional familial or domestic obligations of any kind.[74] When these women, because of their virginal mode of living, also sought a measure of equality in churches that increasingly excluded them, these churches pointed to those very obligations, especially motherhood, as their only route to salvation. While denigrating Eve—the archetypal female, whose punishment for her disobedience to divine order and independent action was the pain of motherhood and submission to the will of her husband—they elevated Mary, who was a mother, but an obedient and a passive one. The virgin-

ity of Mary thus was turned by the church fathers into
a model of purity and obedience, contrasted to the disobedient Eve, who transgressed the divine will while she
was still a virgin. Both were described by patristic authors as opposing "types" of female nature. Justin Martyr
(d. 165), the first to use this typology, asserted in the *Dialogue with Trypho* that, while the virgin Eve "conceived
through the word of the serpent," bringing forth disobedience and death, the virgin Mary conceived through the
Spirit of the Lord, and through her joyful submission,
brought forth obedience and life (*Dialogue* 100.5).

Irenaeus, as previously mentioned, reinforced this typology. As Jean La Porte notes, "The great theologian
of Mary is Irenaeus. . . . Irenaeus completes the parallel
between the two Adams [see Rom. 5:12–21] with a parallel between Eve and Mary. The obedience of Mary is
paralleled with the disobedience of Eve. The two women
appear at the origin of two divine dispensations."[75] Since
Irenaeus's overall design is to refute those Gnostics who
reject "the inheritance of the flesh," he emphasizes Jesus'
human birth from a human woman, but from a woman
who is nevertheless a virgin and an obedient one. Indeed,
Irenaeus sees the birth of Adam as taking place from a
"virgin," the virgin earth (see Tertullian, *On the Flesh of
Christ* 7.14.ff.; Methodius, *Symposium* 3.4), an idea that
makes his theme of virginal "recapitulation" complete:
The first man, Adam, who sinned, is "recapitulated" in
the last man, Christ, who did not; the first woman, Eve,
who was a virgin prior to her disobedience and who by
her disobedience "was made the cause of death, both to
herself and to the whole human race," is recapitulated in
the virgin Mary, who "by yielding obedience, became the
cause of salvation, both to herself and the whole human
race" (*Against Heresies* 3.21–22). Irenaeus does not take
up this argument to claim that Mary is the *savior* of the
whole human race, because to do so would be to deem-
phasize Jesus' role, but it is clear that he believes Mary is
the first who by faith sets in motion the ultimate salvation

of humanity. She is even, for Irenaeus, the comforter and advocate of Eve and the human race (4.33.11), recalling the role of the Paraclete, the comforter and advocate of the disciples after Jesus' death (John 14:25).

Marian doctrine and devotion grew in the churches from the late second century on, continuing the Eve/Mary theme of recapitulation (Tertullian, *On the Flesh of Christ* 17.2ff.; Origen, *Homilies on Matthew* 5; Ephrem Syrus, *On the Nativity* 17.4; *Hymns* 35.17; 49.7; Epiphanius, *Medicine Box* 18). However, the church fathers' discussion of Mary's role in the economy of salvation, like such discussions in the noncanonical texts, seems to have centered almost exclusively upon her virginity, especially as related to her conception and childbearing. In both the Eastern churches, particularly the Syriac-speaking, and the Western churches, which were in general much slower to accord Mary any special devotion, Marian piety increased from the second to the fourth century, precisely in the period of time when monasticism flourished and virginity had an increasingly positive value. By the end of the fourth century, when the monastic movement was at its height, Mary as virgin had become the symbol and model for female celibacy. Ambrose of Milan, the foremost exponent of Mariology in the West, as Ephrem Syrus was in the Syrian East,[76] called Mary the "model" and the "mother" of virgins (*On Virginity* 2.7; 2.15; *Exhortation to Virgins* 27), the "incitement to virginity" (*On the Institution of Virginity* 33), and proclaimed Mary the sinless "first of the redeemed," the beginning of God's work of redemption (*Expositions on Luke* 2.7; 2.17): "Mary... has worked the salvation of the world, and concerned the redemption of all" (*Epistle* 49.2). She helps Christ to defeat the devil (*On the Death of Theodosius* 44). Christians are, like Christ, born of Mary, "an uncorrupt virgin" (*Exposition on Psalm CXVIII* 22.30), who is also the "type" of the church (*Exposition on Luke* 2.7).[77]

The Syrian Orient, even more than the West, valued the commitment to celibacy: A vow of abstinence from marriage and intercourse created an elite within the Syrian churches, the "sons" and "daughters" of the "covenant." Moreover, the Syriac-speaking churches had never had any difficulty producing and employing a rich repertoire of images for the female aspects of the divine, especially the Holy Spirit and Wisdom. It was therefore easy for them to connect Mary, the woman in whom divinity was manifested on earth, to both. In the second-century Syriac *Odes of Solomon* 19, Mary's conception of Jesus by the Holy Spirit appears to offer a powerful contradiction to the assertion of the *Gospel of Philip* that a woman (Mary) cannot conceive by a woman (Spirit). In *Odes* 19, it is the female Holy Spirit who is both the generative principle and the nurturing aspect of the Father (God). It is she who "opens her bosom" and mixes the milk (that which will enable Christ to be conceived) from the Father's "breasts," which are actually her own (19.4–5). It is through this mixture that Mary conceives:

> The womb of the Virgin took (it),
> and she received conception and gave birth.
> (*Odes of Solomon* 6)

Mary's birthing of the Son is without pain, without a midwife (8–9), and empowering:

> She bore as a strong man with desire,
> and she bore according to the manifestation,
> and possessed with great power.
> (*Odes of Solomon* 10)[78]

In the midst of this profusion (and confusion) of images, one thing is clear: Both the Spirit and Mary are mothers, but mothers in a unique, nonsexual, way. Both have powerful roles in imparting salvation to humanity. Both are described by male and female imagery in such a way that earthly gender roles lose definition. Aphrahat, the

Syrian father of the fourth century, identified the Spirit as the mother who "gives birth" to the Christians and especially to celibate Christians (*Demonstrations* 18.840.8–15). Robert Murray has even suggested that, for those churches that conceived of and spoke of the Holy Spirit as female, "a motherly principle in the Trinity [and]... devotion to the person of Mary only grew as this notion declined during the fourth century."[79]

Mary is also identified in Syrian Christianity, both Gnostic and orthodox, with Mary Magdalene.[80] Ephrem Syrus uses "Mary" as a symbol and synonym for virginity:

> It is clear that Virginity is greater
>   and nobler than "Holiness,"
> as for it was she who bore the Son
>   and gave him milk from her breast;
> it was she who sat by his feet
>   and did him service by washing;
> at the cross she was beside him,
>   and in the resurrection she saw him.[81]

Here, "Mary" is identified with the Virgin Mary, Mary of Bethany, and Mary Magdalene. Ephrem, along with other Syrian theologians, linked Mary to the eucharist, which in the "cup of salvation" gives birth to the sacrament as she gave birth, through receiving the Spirit, to the "body of Christ" (Ephrem, *Hymn on the Crucifixion* 3.9; *Hymn on the Unleavened Bread* 6.6–7).[82] Most importantly, however, Mary for the Syrian theologians, as for the Greek and Latin fathers, is the savior of Eve. In the hymns of Cyrillona, for example, Mary is metaphorically described as Eve's daughter, who supports her "crippled" mother in her old age, giving her life, taking away the "leaven of death and pain," so that "all creation might be spared from corruption."[83] Ephrem compares Eve's conception "through the ear" (through hearing) to Mary's conception through receiving the word (*Hymns on the Church* 35.17; *Hymn to the Virgin* 23.5).

Thus we see that Mary became a symbol for a number of concepts in various types of Christianity from the second to the fourth century. Based on what little evidence we have, it appears that women mainly venerated her as mother, a mother not unlike themselves, but a mother who, like Isis, was powerful and empowering, "queen of heaven," giver of life, and perhaps a supporter in the pain of childbirth. Women who adopted and supported a celibate life-style seem not to have employed Mary the Virgin as their own model. Instead, those male theologians who viewed pain in childbirth as a punishment of women for the transgression of Eve either found that childbearing redemptive (e.g., 1 Tim. 2:15) or supported the ideal of Mary's obedience as redeeming the disobedience of Eve. They also appear to have been the ones who, at least by the fourth century, were holding up Mary as the model for female virgins, emphasizing once again her faithful obedience. The more creative Syrian theologians saw Mary not only as the savior of Eve and the model for virgins, male and female, but also as the embodiment of the Holy Spirit, and at times of divine Wisdom. She is also, as mother, the model for the church and for Christians, male and female, who "conceive" the Word (Christ) by the Holy Spirit in a virginal way.[84] However, in all of this literature, while Mary is the "cause of salvation," the "cup of salvation," and the "pure vessel," the passive and obedient receptacle by whom salvation came into the world, rarely is she herself envisioned as being the incarnate savior. Without Mary, there could have been no incarnation: That is probably the reason that orthodox theologians insisted so strenuously upon the reality of Jesus' birth from a real woman. Nevertheless, at the same time they sought to dissociate Mary from the reality of childbirth by an increasing emphasis on her intact and continuing virginity. Thus, the only way in which Mary functioned as redeemer was by ceasing to be fully visualized as a human woman, by being totally dissociated from female sexuality, the "uncleanness of women," in both orthodox and heterodox theology, the former increasingly excluding women from any offices in the churches that would give them authority over men. As women ministered to women in orthodox churches, so also perhaps Mary was designed to be a savior of women: of women only, and not of men. In the final analysis, however, it is indeed Mary who, like Isis and Wisdom, embraces the opposites, in whom virgin and mother, human and divine, spirit and flesh, savior and saved meet.

Notes

1. Michael P. Carroll, *The Cult of the Virgin Mary: Psychological Origins* (Princeton, N.J.: Princeton University Press, 1986), 4.

2. Raymond E. Brown et al., eds., *Mary in the New Testament: A Collaborative Assessment by Protestant and Roman Catholic Scholars* (Philadelphia: Fortress Press, 1978), 293.

3. G. A. Wellen, *Theotokos: Eine ikonographische Abhandlung über das Gottesmutterbild in frühchristliche Zeit* (Utrecht/Antwerp: Spectrum, 1961), 11–14.

4. Brown et al., eds., *Mary*, 58.

5. Ibid., 63; see Jane Schaberg, *The Illegitimacy of Jesus: A Feminist Interpretation of the Infancy Narratives* (San Francisco: Harper & Row, 1987), 163. John 8:41 appears to refer to the charge of illegitimacy against Jesus by his opponents, who claim that *they* are not "illegitimate children."

6. Brown et al., eds., *Mary*, 68–72.

7. Schaberg, *Illegitimacy*, 23.

8. See ibid., 20–34, for a fuller discussion, albeit with a different emphasis, of the role of the four women in Matthew's genealogy.

9. See ibid., 32 n. 58. *Midrash ha-Gadol* 1.334–39 includes Rahab, Ruth, and Bathsheba, but not Tamar.

10. Brown et al., eds., *Mary*, 81.

11. Schaberg, *Illegitimacy*, 22.

12. Ibid., 34.

13. See ibid. for a detailed and insightful feminist approach to this tradition.

14. Paula Fredriksen, *From Jesus to Christ: The Origins of the New Testament Images of Jesus* (New Haven, Conn., and London: Yale University Press, 1988), 43.

15. Brown et al., eds., *Mary*, 92–93.

16. In my acceptance of this interpretation, I reluctantly take issue with Schaberg, *Illegitimacy*, 68–73, whose reading is that Matthew did *not* understand *parthenos* to designate "biological virgin." Her reading of Matthew's "paradoxical" theology is that "the virgin betrothed, seduced, or raped is . . . the virgin who conceives and bears the child they will call Emmanuel" (72–73). I believe that Matthew's emphasis on Mary's virginity in the light of Joseph's suspicion of adultery is a polemical response, perhaps developed in a pre-Matthean stage, to the charge of Jesus' illegitimacy that later surfaced in rabbinic sources (the *Yeshu ben Pantera* traditions in the Talmud and the *Toledoth Yeshu* traditions) and in pagan polemics against Christianity (e.g., Origen, *Against Celsus*). That Matthew would be unlikely to give fuel to such a polemic, responding rather with one of his own, is shown by his allegation that the chief priests bribed the soldiers guarding Jesus' tomb to lie, saying that his disciples stole the body: "And this story is still told among the Jews to this day" (Matt. 28:11–15, NRSV).

17. See Wellen, *Theotokos*, 14–16; and my "The Milk of Salvation: Redemption by the Mother in Late Antiquity and Early Christianity," *HTR* 82/4 (July 1989): 411–12.

18. Brown et al., eds., *Mary*, 134.

19. Ibid., 136.

20. Schaberg, *Illegitimacy*, 97–101. Once again, however, I do not agree with Schaberg that Mary's "humiliation" is caused by the violation of her virginity, although this is much more likely to fit into Luke's theological scheme than Matthew's.

21. Brown et al., eds., *Mary*, 143; see Schaberg, *Illegitimacy*, 100–101.

22. If the Song of Mary represents this Ebionite theology, or one similar to it, it seems to me even more unlikely, pace Schaberg, that Luke would have accented or regarded Mary as a violated virgin; see Schaberg, *Illegitimacy*, 97–101.

23. Brown et al., eds., *Mary*, 144.

24. Raymond Brown, *The Birth of the Messiah* (Garden City, N.Y.: Doubleday/Image, 1979), 416–17, on the other hand, believes that Luke is deliberately contrasting the rebellion of the messianic "pretender," Judas the Galilean, which occurred in 6 C.E. as a result of the census, with the birth of the peaceful messiah, Jesus. Although this contrast would fit in with Luke's

general disposition to show Christians as good citizens of the
Roman world, it nevertheless does not preclude the suggestion
that the "Roman peace" might be maintained by oppressive
means. Brown does, however, point out that Luke sets the birth
of Jesus "against the background of the imperial claims of Augustus," who was portrayed as having established this imperial
peace (420).

25. Tal. Bab. *Sanhedrin* 25b (cited in Brown, *Birth*, 420 n. 38).

26. Gerd Theissen, *The Social Setting of Pauline Christianity*,
ed. and trans. John H. Schütz (Philadelphia: Fortress Press,
1982), 33.

27. Brown, *Birth*, 437, commentary on Luke 2:23.

28. Brown et al., eds., *Mary*, 156–57.

29. Schaberg, *Illegitimacy*, 142; Brown et al., eds., *Mary*, 151.

30. Elisabeth Schüssler Fiorenza, *In Memory of Her: A Feminist Theological Reconstruction of Christian Origins* (New York:
Crossroad, 1983), 146; see Schaberg, *Illegitimacy*, 142.

31. Schaberg, *Illegitimacy*, 144.

32. See Brown, *Birth*, 244–53.

33. Brown et al., eds., *Mary*, 179 n. 405.

34. Ibid., 216.

35. Robert T. Fortna, *The Gospel of Signs*, SNTSMS, 11 (Cambridge: Cambridge University Press, 1970), 38 (cited in Brown
et al., eds., *Mary*, 184–85).

36. Brown et al., eds., *Mary*, 188.

37. Ibid., 189.

38. Ibid., 193.

39. Raymond E. Brown, *The Community of the Beloved Disciple*
(New York: Paulist Press, 1979), 195.

40. Brown et al., eds., *Mary*, 213, 216.

41. Docetism is the belief that Jesus only appeared to be
flesh, but actually was spirit. See Brown, *Community*, for the
point of view of the Johannine "secessionists," and the response
to them by the author of 1 John, who possibly edited the Gospel
of John.

42. Susan Ashbrook Harvey, "Women in Early Syriac Christianity," in *Images of Women in Antiquity*, ed. Averil Cameron and
Amélie Kuhrt (Detroit: Wayne State University Press, 1983),
290.

43. Bentley Layton, trans., *The Gnostic Scriptures* (Garden
City, N.Y.: Doubleday, 1987), 360–65.

44. Harvey, "Women," 291.

45. Ibid.

46. C. H. Roberts, *Catalogue of the Greek and Latin Papyri in the John Rylands Library* 3 (1938): 46ff. (cited by Hilda Graef, *Mary: A History of Doctrine and Devotion* [New York: Sheed & Ward, 1963], 1:48).

47. Trans. Ross S. Kraemer, *Maenads, Martyrs, Matrons, and Monastics: A Sourcebook on Women's Religions in the Greco-Roman World* (Philadelphia: Fortress Press, 1988), 50, no. 29.

48. Oscar Cullmann, "Infancy Gospels," in Edgar Hennecke, *New Testament Apocrypha*, vol. 1: *Gospels and Related Writings*, ed. Wilhelm Schneemelcher; Eng. trans. ed. R. McL. Wilson (Philadelphia: Westminster Press, 1963), 368.

49. Rosemary R. Ruether, *Mary, the Feminine Face of the Church* (Philadelphia: Westminster Press, 1977), 50.

50. Ibid., 58–60.

51. Graef, *Mary*, 1:35.

52. Brown et al., eds., *Mary*, 233; see Ruether, *Mary*, 27.

53. Carroll, *Cult*, 5.

54. *Gospel of Thomas*, logion 101, trans. Layton, *Gnostic Scriptures*, 380–409.

55. Trans. Layton, *Gnostic Scriptures;* modified. Brackets are mine, and represent suggested readings, not gaps.

56. Trans. Layton, *Gnostic Scriptures*.

57. Ibid., 325.

58. Trans. Layton, *Gnostic Scriptures*. "Powers" is an alternate suggestion for "forces."

59. See ibid., 332 nn. 14a and 14b.

60. Trans. R. McL. Wilson, *The Nag Hammadi Library in English*, ed. James M. Robinson (San Francisco: Harper & Row, 1977).

61. See Jorunn Jacobsen Buckley, "The Holy Spirit Is a Double Name," in *Images of the Feminine in Gnosticism*, ed. Karen L. King, Studies in Antiquity and Christianity (Philadelphia: Fortress Press, 1988), 218–19.

62. Cullmann, "Infancy Gospels," 374.

63. *Acts of Archelaus* 54. Epiphanius has a version of this "heresy" that is indicative of both the reason why Manicheans rejected the birth from Mary and what he may have thought about natural physical birth: "Now their vain labor went so far that they did not admit that the Only-Begotten, the Christ who

had come down from the bosom of the Father, was the son of a certain woman named Mary, born of flesh and blood and the other uncleanness of women" (*Medicine Box* 66.6.9 [cited in Brown et al., eds., *Mary*, 269 n. 615]).

64. Cullmann, "Infancy Gospels," 373–75.

65. Trans. in ANF, 16:515–20.

66. Ibid.

67. *The Miracles of Mary*, in E. A. W. Budge, trans., *The History of the Blessed Virgin* (London, 1899), 47, 51–52, 59–67.

68. See Virginia Burrus, *Chastity as Autonomy* (Berkeley, Calif.: Graduate Theological Union, 1989); and my "The Divine Woman: A Reconsideration," *ATR* 70/3 (July 1988): 207–20.

69. Tertullian, *On Baptism* 17.

70. Beatrice Beaulieu, "The Image of the Virgin Mother," in *Women and Religion*, ed. Judith Plaskow and Joan Arnold, Aids for the Study of Religion (Missoula, Mont.: Scholars Press, 1974), 93–104. I disagree with Beaulieu's statement that "an image of feminine nature need not be limited in its significance to being an image of women, designed to provide for social and psychological needs" (93). Female images always reflect actual women and how they and others perceive them, thus providing for those exact needs.

71. See my "Milk of Salvation," 411; Wellen, *Theotokos*, 14–16; Robert Javelet, "Marie, la femme médiatrice," *RevScRel* 58 (1984): 165.

72. See Victor Tran Tam Tinh, *Isis Lactans*, EPRO, 26 (Leiden: E. J. Brill, 1973), 45.

73. Carroll, *Cult*, 19.

74. Rosemary R. Ruether, *Women-Church: Theology and Practice of Feminist Liberation Communities* (San Francisco: Harper & Row, 1985), 13–14.

75. Jean La Porte, *The Role of Women in Early Christianity*, Studies in Women and Religion, 7 (New York and Toronto: Edwin Mellen Press, 1982), 152.

76. Graef, *Mary*, 1:88.

77. All translations are from ibid., 82–84.

78. Trans. James H. Charlesworth, *The Odes of Solomon* (Oxford: Clarendon, 1973), 81.

79. Robert Murray, "Mary the Second Eve in the Early Syriac Fathers," *Eastern Church Review* 3/4 (1971): 373.

80. Robert Murray, *Symbols of Church and Kingdom: A Study in Early Syriac Tradition* (Cambridge: Cambridge University Press, 1975), 147–48, 330–33.

81. Ibid., 330.

82. Murray, "Mary the Second Eve," 373–84; see Sebastian Brock, "Mary and the Eucharist: An Oriental Perspective," *Sobornost* 1/2 (1979): 50–59.

83. Murray, "Mary the Second Eve," 377.

84. Brock, "Mary and the Eucharist," 59.

Epilogue

We began this investigation with two related questions: Can a male savior save women? and, Why must the savior be male? For many Christian women, both in the present and in the past, the image of the savior as male has presented problems for self-orientation and self-identity. The portrayal of the agent of God's salvation as embodied in a particular male, Jesus of Nazareth, and the emphasis upon Jesus' gender were not mere historical accidents, but resulted from a culturally limited process of selection that excluded other possible embodiments. We have examined three possible models of the savior—the universal savior, the mediator between the divine and human realms, and the incarnate redeemer—and have suggested how these three models might have been portrayed as female rather than male, how women may have responded to them, and what these savior figures may tell us about women's own experiences.

The scarcity of the evidence has made it difficult in each case to discover what women's responses to Isis, Sophia, and Mary may have been, since women's voices, especially when describing their own experiences, have been silenced by the same process of selectivity that made women as savior figures invisible. Nevertheless, what evidence can be uncovered seems to indicate that women saw in female savior figures both an embodiment and an exaltation of those experiences particular to their own lives, especially that of motherhood. Isis saves, in fact, because she is a mother, the giver and sustainer of life.

Sophia is embodied in the "mothers in Israel," who give wise and saving counsel to spouses, children, and even kings. Mary, like Isis, combines various stages of women's lives, but is also a mother of salvation, and, like Sophia, is a mediator between the divine and human realms precisely through her conception and childbearing.

Thus it may be said that women valued in female saviors the very things that men devalued and portrayed as "limits": female sexuality and bodiliness. For males, the generators and selectors of the dominant images of the savior, women, like men, needed to be saved *from* the limits of the body: Indeed, for men, women became identified *with* the body. Thus, for Christian male writers, Jesus as the universal savior incarnated power *over* life and death, the power of the male deity who saved through word and deed rather than through giving birth and rebirth. Sophia, first embodied in the wise women and mothers of Israel, became incarnate in the written Torah and later the male sage, the Torah being his exclusive province. Jesus, originally seen as the messenger of Sophia, was later envisioned as her only embodiment. Finally, in the New Testament and later Christian writers, the biological motherhood of Mary, Jesus' mother, is deemphasized, whereas her virginity and her obedience are selected as two models for Christian women to follow.

We thus can answer our second question first: In the writings of formative Christianity, the savior *must* be male; only so can he rescue humanity from its limits, especially the limit of human embodiment and human disobedience, often portrayed as "the works of the female." Women can be saved only if they are either obedient (to males, the male savior, the male God) or if they themselves deny their embodiment as females and "make themselves male." Can a male savior save women? It depends on who is responding to the question. Certainly Christian writers, almost exclusively men, thought the male Jesus was the only route of salvation for women, disobedient and unruly as was the female nature of humanity, symbolized and embodied in Eve. But the voices of some Christian women, though muted and almost erased by time, offer us a different answer—like that given by the Arabian women of Thracian descent who offered the worship of women to a woman savior.

Select Bibliography

Arthur, Rose Horman. *The Wisdom Goddess*. Lanham, Md.: University Press of America, 1984.

Aschkenasy, Nehama. *Eve's Journey: Feminine Images in Hebraic Literary Tradition*. Philadelphia: University of Pennsylvania Press, 1986.

Atkinson, Clarissa W., Constance W. Buchanan, and Margaret R. Miles, eds. *Immaculate and Powerful: The Female in Sacred Image and Social Reality*. Boston: Beacon Press, 1985.

Baer, Richard A. *Philo's Use of the Categories Male and Female*. Leiden: E. J. Brill, 1970.

Banta, Martha L. *Imaging American Women: Idea and Ideals in Cultural History*. New York: Columbia University Press, 1987.

Bergmann, J. *Ich bin Isis: Studien zum memphitischen Hintergrund der griechischen Isisaretalogien*. Stockholm: Almqvist and Wiksell, 1968.

Berry, Wanda Warren. "Images of Sin and Salvation in Feminist Theology." *ATR* 60/1 (January 1978): 25–54.

Bieler, Ludwig. *THEIOS ANER*. 1935–36. Reprint. Darmstadt: Wissenschaftliche Buchgesellschaft, 1967.

Boucher, Madeleine. "Some Unexplored Parallels to 1 Cor. 11:11–12 and Gal. 3:28: The NT on the Role of Women." *CBQ* 31 (1969): 50–58.

Brandon, S. G. F., ed. *The Saviour God: Comparative Studies in the Concept of Salvation: Presented to Edwin Oliver James*. Manchester: Manchester University Press, 1963.

Brock, Sebastian. "Mary and the Eucharist: An Oriental Perspective." *Sobornost* 1/2 (1979): 50–59.

Brooten, Bernadette. "Feminist Perspectives on New Testament Exegesis." *Concilium* 138 (1980): 55–61.

Brown, Peter. *The Body and Society: Men, Women, and Sexual Renunciation in Early Christianity.* New York: Columbia University Press, 1988.
————. *The Making of Late Antiquity.* Cambridge, Mass.: Harvard University Press, 1978.
Brown, Raymond E. *The Birth of the Messiah.* Garden City, N.Y.: Doubleday/Image Books, 1979.
————. *The Community of the Beloved Disciple.* New York: Paulist Press, 1979.
Brown, Raymond E., et al., eds. *Mary in the New Testament: A Collaborative Assessment by Protestant and Roman Catholic Scholars.* Philadelphia: Fortress Press, 1978.
Budge, E. A. W., trans. *The History of the Blessed Virgin.* London, 1899.
Bultmann, Rudolf. *Jesus Christ and Mythology.* London: SCM Press, 1961.
Burkert, Walter. *Ancient Mystery Cults.* Cambridge, Mass.: Harvard University Press, 1987.
Burrus, Virginia. *Chastity as Autonomy.* Berkeley, Calif.: Graduate Theological Union, 1989.
————. "Chastity as Autonomy: Women in the Stories of the Apocryphal Acts." In *The Apocryphal Acts of the Apostles,* edited by Dennis R. MacDonald, 101–18. Semeia, 38. Decatur, Ga.: Scholars Press, 1986.
Bynum, Caroline Walker, Stevan Harrell, and Paula Richman, eds. *Gender and Religion: On the Complexity of Symbols.* Boston: Beacon Press, 1986.
Cameron, Averil. "Neither Male Nor Female." *Greece and Rome* 27 (1977): 60–68.
————. "The Theotokos in Sixth-Century Constantinople." *Journal of Theological Studies,* n.s., 29/1 (April 1978): 79–108.
Cameron, Averil, and Amélie Kuhrt, eds. *Images of Women in Antiquity.* Detroit: Wayne State University Press, 1983.
Camp, Claudia V. "Female Sage and Biblical Wisdom." Paper presented to the Male and Female in Gnosticism Section, AAR/SBL Annual Meeting, Chicago, Ill., November 17–20, 1988.
————. *Wisdom and the Feminine in the Book of Proverbs.* Bible and Literature Series, 11. Sheffield: JSOT/Almond Press, 1985.
Cantarella, Eva. *Pandora's Daughters: The Role and Status of Women in Greek and Roman Antiquity.* Translated by Mau-

reen B. Fant. Baltimore: Johns Hopkins University Press, 1987.

Carroll, Michael P. *The Cult of the Virgin Mary: Psychological Origins*. Princeton, N.J.: Princeton University Press, 1986.

Charlesworth, James H., trans. *The Odes of Solomon*. Oxford: Clarendon Press, 1973.

Clark, Elizabeth A. "Ascetic Renunciation and Feminine Advancement: A Paradox of Late Ancient Christianity." *ATR* 63 (1981): 240–57.

Cohen, Shaye. *From the Maccabees to the Mishnah*. Library of Early Christianity. Philadelphia: Westminster Press, 1987.

Corrington, Gail Paterson. *The "Divine Man": His Origin and Function in Hellenistic Popular Religion*. American University Studies, 8:17. Bern and New York: Peter Lang, 1986.

———. "The Divine Woman: A Reconsideration." *ATR* 70/3 (July 1988): 207–20.

———. "The Divine Woman? Propaganda and the Power of Chastity in the New Testament Apocrypha." *Helios*, n.s., 13/1 (1986): 151–62.

———. "The Milk of Salvation: Redemption by the Mother in Late Antiquity and Early Christianity." *HTR* 82/4 (July 1989): 393–420.

———. "Power and the Man of Power in Hellenistic Popular Belief." *Helios*, n.s., 13/2 (1986): 75–86.

Craven, Toni. *Artistry and Faith in the Book of Judith*. SBLDS, 70. Chico, Calif.: Scholars Press, 1983.

Daly, Mary. *Beyond God the Father: Toward a Philosophy of Women's Liberation*. Boston: Beacon Press, 1973.

———. *The Church and the Second Sex*. Boston: Beacon Press, 1985.

Davies, Stevan. *The Revolt of the Widows: The Social World of the Apocryphal Acts*. Carbondale, Ill.: University of Illinois Press, 1980.

Denton, R. C. "Redeem, Redeemer, Redemption." *IDB* 4:21–22.

Diel, Paul. *The God-Symbol: Its History and Its Significance*. Translated by Nelly Marans. San Francisco: Harper & Row, 1986.

Douglas, Mary. *Natural Symbols: Explorations in Cosmology*. New York: Pantheon Books/Random House, 1970.

Dunand, Françoise. *Religion populaire en Égypte romaine: Les ter-res cuites isiaques au Musée du Caire*. EPRO, 66. Leiden: E. J. Brill, 1979.

———. "Le statut des *hiereiai* en Égypte romaine." In *Hom-mages à Martin Vermaseren*, vol. 1, edited by M. B. de Boer and T. A. Edridge, 352–75. Leiden: E. J. Brill, 1978.

Eliade, Mircea. *A History of Religious Ideas*. Vol. 2: *From Gautama Buddha to the Triumph of Christianity*. Chicago: University of Chicago Press, 1982.

Euripides. Vol. 4 of *The Complete Greek Tragedies*, edited by David Grene and Richmond Lattimore. Chicago: University of Chicago Press, 1958.

Festugière, A. J. "À propos des arètalogies d'Isis." *HTR* 42/4 (1949): 209–304.

Fischer-Mueller, Aydeet. "The Gnostic Sophia: Suffering Sis-ter of Hokhmah and Eve." Paper presented to the Male and Female in Gnosticism Section, AAR/SBL Annual Meeting, Chicago, Ill., November 17–20, 1988.

Fohrer, G., and W. Foerster. "Sozo." *TDNT* 7:965–1024.

Fortna, Robert T. *The Gospel of Signs*. SNTSMS, 11. Cambridge: Cambridge University Press, 1970.

Frankfort, Henri. *Kingship and the Gods*. Chicago: University of Chicago Press, 1948.

Fredriksen, Paula. *From Jesus to Christ: The Origins of the New Testament Images of Jesus*. New Haven, Conn., and London: Yale University Press, 1988.

Gager, John G. "Body-Symbols and Social Reality: Resurrec-tion, Incarnation, and Asceticism in Early Christianity." *Re-ligion* 12 (1982): 345–63.

Geertz, Clifford, "Religion as a Cultural System." In *Anthropo-logical Approaches to the Study of Religion*, edited by Michael Banton, 1–46. London and New York: Tavistock Publica-tions, 1966.

Goldenberg, Naomi. *The Changing of the Gods*. Boston: Beacon Press, 1979.

Good, Deirdre. *Reconstructing the Traditions of Sophia*. SBLMS, 32. Atlanta, Ga.: Scholars Press, 1987.

Graef, Hilda. *Mary: A History of Doctrine and Devotion*. 2 vols. New York: Sheed & Ward, 1963.

Grant, F. C. *Hellenistic Religions*. New York: Liberal Arts Press, 1953.

Green, Henry A. "The Socio-economic Background of Christianity in Egypt." In *The Roots of Egyptian Christianity*, edited by Birger A. Pearson and James E. Goehring, 100–113. Studies in Antiquity and Christianity. Philadelphia: Fortress Press, 1986.

Grene, David, and Richmond Lattimore. *Greek Tragedies*. Vol. 1. Chicago: University of Chicago Press, 1966.

Hadas, Moses, and Morton Smith. *Heroes and Gods: Spiritual Biographies in Antiquity*. Religious Perspectives, 13. New York: Harper & Row, 1965.

Haerens, H. "Soter et soteria." *Studia hellenistica* 5 (1948): 57–68.

Hennecke, Edgar. *New Testament Apocrypha*. Vol. 1: *Gospels and Related Writings*, edited by Wilhelm Schneemelcher. English translation edited by R. McL. Wilson. Philadelphia: Westminster Press, 1963.

Heschel, Susannah, ed. *On Being a Jewish Feminist*. New York: Schocken Books, 1983.

Heyob, Sharon Kelly. *The Cult of Isis Among Women in the Greco-Roman World*. EPRO, 51. Leiden: E. J. Brill, 1975.

Javelet, Robert. "Marie, la femme médiatrice." *RevScRel* 58 (1984): 162–71.

King, Karen L., ed. *Images of the Feminine in Gnosticism*. Studies in Antiquity and Christianity. Philadelphia: Fortress Press, 1989.

Kloppenborg, John. "Isis and Sophia in the Book of Wisdom." *HTR* 75 (1982): 57–84.

Kraemer, Ross S. "The Conversion of Women to Ascetic Forms of Christianity." *Signs* 6 (1980): 298–307.

———, ed. *Maenads, Martyrs, Matrons, and Monastics: A Sourcebook on Women's Religions in the Greco-Roman World*. Philadelphia: Fortress Press, 1988.

Langer, Susanne K. *Philosophy in a New Key: A Study in the Symbolism of Reason, Rite, and Art*. Cambridge, Mass.: Harvard University Press, 1942.

La Porte, Jean. *The Role of Women in Early Christianity*. Studies in Women and Religion, 7. New York and Toronto: Edwin Mellen Press, 1982.

Layton, Bentley, ed. and trans. *The Gnostic Scriptures*. Garden City, N.Y.: Doubleday, 1987.

Leclant, Jean. *Inventaire Bibliographique des Isiaca (IBIS)*. EPRO, 18. Leiden: E. J. Brill, 1972–74.

———. "Le rôle d'allaîtement d'après les textes des Pyramides." *JNES* 10 (1951): 123–27.

Le Corsu, France. *Isis: Mythe et Mystères*. Paris: Les "Belles Lettres," 1977.

Lefkowitz, Mary R. *Women in Greek Myth*. Baltimore: Johns Hopkins University Press, 1986.

Lefkowitz, Mary R., and Maureen B. Fant. *Women's Life in Greece and Rome: A Source Book in Translation*. Baltimore: Johns Hopkins University Press, 1982.

Long, A. A., ed. *Problems in Stoicism*. London: University of London Press/Athlone Press, 1971.

Lyonnet, S., and L. Sabourin, eds. *Sin, Redemption, and Sacrifice*. Analecta biblica, 48. Rome: Biblical Institute Press, 1970.

Maccoby, Hyam. *The Mythmaker: Paul and the Invention of Christianity*. New York: Harper & Row, 1986.

McFague, Sallie. *Metaphorical Theology: Models of God in Religious Language*. Philadelphia: Fortress Press, 1981.

Mack, Burton. *Logos und Sophia: Untersuchungen zur Weisheitstheologie im hellenistischen Judentum*. Studien zur Umwelt des Neuen Testaments, 10. Göttingen: Vandenhoeck & Ruprecht, 1973.

———. "Q and Christian Origins." In *Early Christianity, Jesus, and Q*. Semeia, 54. Atlanta: Scholars Press, forthcoming.

McNamara, JoAnn. "Sexual Equality and the Cult of Virginity in Early Christian Thought." *Feminist Studies* 3 (1976): 145–58.

MacRae, George W. "The Jewish Background of the Sophia Myth." *Novum Testamentum* 12 (1970): 86–101.

Martin, Luther H. *Hellenistic Religions*. New York: Oxford University Press, 1988.

Meeks, Wayne. "The Image of the Androgyne." *HR* 13 (1974): 165–208.

Meyers, Carol. *Discovering Eve: Ancient Israelite Women in Context*. New York: Oxford University Press, 1988.

———. "The Roots of Restriction: Women in Early Israel." *Biblical Archaeologist* 41 (1978): 91–102.

Miles, Margaret R. *Carnal Knowing*. Boston: Beacon Press, 1989.

————. *Image as Insight: Visual Understanding in Western Christianity and Secular Culture*. Boston: Beacon Press, 1985.

Minear, Paul. *Images of the Church in the New Testament*. Philadelphia: Westminster Press, 1966.

Moore, Carey A. *Judith: A New Translation with Introduction, Notes, and Commentary*. Anchor Bible. Garden City, N.Y.: Doubleday, 1985.

Murray, Robert. "Mary the Second Eve in the Early Syriac Fathers." *Eastern Church Review* 3/4 (1971): 372–84.

————. *Symbols of Church and Kingdom: A Study in Early Syriac Tradition*. Cambridge: Cambridge University Press, 1975.

The Nag Hammadi Library in English. Edited by James M. Robinson. San Francisco: Harper & Row, 1977.

Neusner, Jacob. *The Incarnation of God: The Character of Divinity in Formative Judaism*. Philadelphia: Fortress Press, 1988.

Neusner, Jacob, William Scott Green, and Ernest Frerichs, eds. *Judaisms and Their Messiahs at the Turn of the Christian Era*. Cambridge and New York: Cambridge University Press, 1987.

Nickelsburg, George W. *Jewish Literature Between the Bible and the Mishnah*. Philadelphia: Fortress Press, 1981.

Nilsson, Martin P. *Greek Popular Religion*. New York: Columbia University Press, 1940.

Nunn, Madelan. "Christology or Male-olatry?" *Duke Divinity School Review* 42/3 (1977): 143–48.

Ochshorn, Judith. *The Female Experience and the Nature of the Divine*. Bloomington, Ind.: Indiana University Press, 1981.

Owens, Craig R. "The Discourse of Others: Feminists and Post-modernism." In *The Anti-aesthetic: Essays in Post-modern Culture*, edited by Hal Foster, 57–77. Port Townsend, Wash.: Bag Press, 1983.

Pagels, Elaine. *The Gnostic Gospels*. New York: Random House, 1979.

————. "Whatever Became of God the Mother?" In *The Signs Reader: Women, Gender, and Scholarship*, edited by Elizabeth Abel and Emily K. Abel, 97–107. Chicago: University of Chicago Press, 1989.

Pearson, Birger A. *Philo and the Gnostics on Man and Salvation*. Protocol of the 29th Colloquy of the Center for Hermeneutical Studies in Hellenistic and Modern Culture, 17 April

1977. Berkeley, Calif.: Graduate Theological Union and University of California Press, 1977.

Plaskow, Judith, and Joan Arnold, eds. *Women and Religion.* Aids for the Study of Religion. Missoula, Mont.: Scholars Press, 1974.

Pomeroy, Sarah. *Goddesses, Whores, Wives, and Slaves: Women in Classical Antiquity.* New York: Schocken Books, 1975.

Price, Theodora Hadzisteliou. *Kourotrophos: Cults and Representations of Greek Nursing Deities.* Leiden: E. J. Brill, 1978.

Rice, David G., and John E. Stambaugh. *Sources for the Study of Greek Religion.* Sources for Biblical Study, 14. Missoula, Mont.: Scholars Press, 1979.

Richardson, Alan. "Salvation, Savior." *IDB* 4:168–81.

Robinson, James M., and Helmut Koester. *Trajectories Through Early Christianity.* Philadelphia: Fortress Press, 1971.

Rosaldo, Michelle Zimbalist, and Louise Lamphere, eds. *Women, Culture, and Society.* Stanford, Calif.: Stanford University Press, 1974.

Ruether, Rosemary R. *Mary, The Feminine Face of the Church.* Philadelphia: Westminster Press, 1977.

————. "Mothers of the Church: Ascetic Women in the Late Patristic Age." In *Women of Spirit: Female Leadership in the Jewish and Christian Traditions,* edited by Rosemary R. Ruether and Eleanor McLaughlin, 71–98. New York: Simon & Schuster, 1979.

————. *Sexism and God-Talk: Toward a Feminist Theology.* Boston: Beacon Press, 1983.

————. *Women-Church: Theology and Practice of Feminist Liberation Communities.* San Francisco: Harper & Row, 1985.

————. *Womanguides: Readings Toward a Feminist Theology.* Boston: Beacon Press, 1985.

————, ed. *Religion and Sexism: Images of Women in the Jewish and Christian Traditions.* New York: Simon & Schuster, 1974.

Sawyer, John F. A. *Semantics in Biblical Research.* Studies in Biblical Theology, 2d series, 24. Naperville, Ill.: Alec R. Allenson, 1972.

Schaberg, Jane. *The Illegitimacy of Jesus: A Feminist Interpretation of the Infancy Narratives.* San Francisco: Harper & Row, 1987.

Schüssler Fiorenza, Elisabeth. *In Memory of Her: A Feminist Theological Reconstruction of Christian Origins.* New York: Crossroad, 1983.

————. *Theological Criteria and Historical Reconstruction: Martha and Mary in Luke 10:38–42*. Protocol of the 53rd Colloquy of the Center for Hermeneutical Studies, 10 April 1986. Berkeley, Calif.: Graduate Theological Union and the University of California Press, 1987.

————. "Word and Spirit and Power: Women in Early Christian Communities." In *Women of Spirit: Female Leadership in the Jewish and Christian Traditions*, edited by Rosemary R. Ruether and Eleanor McLaughlin, 29–70. New York: Simon & Schuster, 1979.

Scott, Joan W. "Gender: A Useful Category of Historical Analysis." *American Historical Review* 91/5 (1984): 1053–75.

Sharpe, Eric J., and John R. Hinnells, eds. *Man and His Salvation: Studies in Honor of S. G. F. Brandon*. Manchester: Manchester University Press, 1973.

Smid, H. R. *Protevangelium Jacobi: A Commentary*. Assen: Van Gorcum, 1965.

Swidler, Leonard R. "Jesus Was a Feminist." *Catholic World* 214 (1971): 177–83.

Talbert, Charles H. "The Myth of a Descending-ascending Redeemer in Mediterranean Antiquity." *NTS* 22 (1976): 418–39.

Taussig, Hal. "Sophia and Her Children in Q." Paper presented to the Male and Female in Gnosticism Section, AAR/SBL Annual Meeting, Chicago, Ill., November 17–20, 1988.

Theissen, Gerd. *The Social Setting of Pauline Christianity*. Edited, translated, and introduced by John H. Schütz. Philadelphia: Fortress Press, 1982.

————. *The Sociology of Early Palestinian Christianity*. Philadelphia: Fortress Press, 1978.

Tillich, Paul. *Systematic Theology*. Vol. 3. Chicago: University of Chicago Press, 1963.

Totti, Maria. *Ausgewählte Texte der Isis-und-Sarapis Religion*. Subsidia epigraphica, 12. Hildesheim: Georg Olms, 1985.

Tran Tam Tinh, Victor. *Isis Lactans*. EPRO, 26. Leiden: E. J. Brill, 1973.

Trible, Phyllis. *God and the Rhetoric of Sexuality*. Philadelphia: Fortress Press, 1978.

————. *Texts of Terror*. Philadelphia: Fortress Press, 1985.

Vidman, Ladislaus. *Sylloge inscriptionum religionis Isiacae et Sarapicae*. Berlin: Walter de Gruyter, 1969.

Warner, Marina. *Alone of All Her Sex: The Myth and Cult of the Virgin Mary*. New York: Alfred A. Knopf, 1976.

Wellen, G. A. *Theotokos: Eine ikonographische Abhandlung über das Gottesmutterbild in frühchristliche Zeit*. Utrecht/Antwerp: Spectrum, 1961.

Wilken, Robert L., ed. *Aspects of Wisdom in Judaism and Early Christianity*. Notre Dame, Ind.: University of Notre Dame Press, 1975.

Wilson-Kastner, Patricia. *A Lost Tradition: Women Writers of the Early Church*. Lanham, Md.: University Press of America, 1981.

Witt, R. E. "The Importance of Isis for the Fathers." *Studia patristica*, 8. *Texte und Untersuchungen zur Geschichte der altchristlichen Literatur* 93 (1966): 134–45.

———. "Isis-Hellas." *Proceedings of the Cambridge Philological Society*, n.s., 12 (1966): 48–69.

———. *Isis in the Greco-Roman World*. London: Thames & Hudson, 1971.

Index